Muckrakers

Ann Bausum
Foreword by Daniel Schorr, NPR Senior News Analyst

16pt

Copyright Page from the Original Book

Text copyright © 2007 Ann Bausum
Published by the National Geographic Society.
All rights reserved. Reproduction of the whole or any part of the contents without written permission from the National Geographic Society is strictly prohibited.

Library of Congress Cataloging-in-Publication Data
Bausum, Ann.
  Muckrakers : how Ida Tarbell, Upton Sinclair, and Lincoln Steffens helped expose scandal, inspire reform, and invent investigative journalism / by Ann Bausum.
    p. cm.
  Includes bibliographical references and index.
  ISBN 978-1-4263-0137-7 (trade : alk. paper) — ISBN 978-1-4263-0138-4 (library : alk. paper)
  1. Investigative reporting—United States—History—20th century. 2. Tarbell, Ida M. (Ida Minerva), 1857-1944. 3. Sinclair, Upton, 1878-1968. 4. Steffens, Lincoln, 1866-1936. I. Title.
  PN4888.I56B38 2007
  070.4'30973—dc22
                                                    2007011391

Printed in the United States of America

A Note on Design

The design of this book pays tribute to two tools of the muckraking trade from 100 years ago: black-and-white photography and the typewriter. At the beginning of the 20th century, photographers relied on glass plate negatives to produce their photographs. Often photographers scratched a brief description, date, or record number directly onto a plate. These captions appeared on prints from the plates and helped identify the images. That tradition inspired the use in this book of brief superimposed captions on many photographs.

Antique typewriter keys introduce this book's chapters, serve as its page numbers, and grace its covers. The opening page of each chapter mimics the look of a typewritten manuscript. So do the book's photo captions. Copy that could be italicized using a computer today is shown underlined in these sections, just like it would have been a century ago. In those days, underlined text had to be typed twice—once to show the letters, and once to add the underlining strokes. The backspace key was indispensable for this task. The final page of this book encourages readers to go back and take a second look at its pages.

Text is set in Filosophia by Emigre. Display fonts are Houston Pen, Slab American, Trixie and Dear Sarah.

TABLE OF CONTENTS

Foreword	ii
Introduction	vii
Chapter 1: THE SHAME OF THE NATION	1
Chapter 2: MUCKRAKER ORIGINS	11
Chapter 3: FIGHTING THE OCTOPUS	25
Chapter 4: LABOR AND LAMB CHOPS	39
Chapter 5: SHAKING THE FOUNDATIONS	55
Chapter 6: AN ENDURING TRADITION	73
Afterword	87
Time Line of Muckraking and Pantheon of Muckrakers	98
Resource Guide	135
Bibliography	138
Research Notes and Acknowledgments	143
Citations and Illustrations Credits	150
Front Cover Flap	163
Back Cover Flap	165
Back Cover Material	168
Index	169

For my brother David: first hero, first friend, first to introduce me to the muckrakers.

Foreword

Daniel Schorr testified before the House Ethics Committee in 1976. The committee threatened him with jail for contempt of Congress if he did not reveal a source. He refused, saying, "to betray a source would mean to dry up many future sources for many future reporters.... It would mean betraying myself, my career, and my life."

They were called muckrakers then. They are called investigative reporters now. They were named Ida Tarbell, Upton Sinclair, and Lincoln Steffens then. They are named Seymour Hersh, Dana Priest, and Woodward and

Bernstein now. But now as then, going where more timorous journalists fear to tread, they make a vital contribution to the health of our society by exposing some of the corruption that creeps into government and business.

My admiration for investigative reporters (most of them, in Washington, are friends of mine) is the greater because, in younger days, I tried to emulate them, with only moderate success. But, I learned that, for a journalist, there is no greater thrill than seeing the concrete effects of laying bare evil.

At the age of 90, I look back to the story that brought down a Presidency—Watergate. As the chief Watergate correspondent for CBS, I played a small part in uncovering the Nixon conspiracy. You may know that it was mainly the work of *Washington Post* reporters Bob Woodward and Carl Bernstein. But it was a small thrill to learn that when the bill of impeachment against Nixon was written, I was named as a target of his abuse of presidential powers, because he had ordered the FBI to spy on me.

In the Congressional investigation of CIA misdeeds that became known as "son of Watergate," I exposéd the agency's plans to assassinate Cuban leader Fidel Castro. And I reveled in the sense of having made a contribution to reforming the CIA.

But the quintessential investigative feat, because it had such a profound effect on forcing Americans to see their sometimes-gratuitous violence, was Sy Hersh's exposure of the My Lai massacre in Vietnam. The best investigative reports are those that force us to come to terms with our failings.

In appearances on college campuses in the years after Watergate, I have constantly been asked how to become a famous journalist like Woodward or Bernstein. So, for those who may aspire to follow in the footsteps of our journalistic heroes, I have a word of advice: The journalistic task today is not to try to imitate Watergate, but to examine the situations today that need to be exposéd. Today's Watergate may be the abuse of Iraqi prisoners in Abu Ghraib. Or the mistreatment of American soldiers in the Walter Reed

Army Medical Center. Or the neglect of the homeless in some communities.

I commend National Geographic for its initiative in devoting this book to our past journalistic heroes. I hope it will inspire some future muckrakers to help clean up our society.

Daniel Schorr

Daniel Schorr
NPB Senior News Analyst

Wanted: President Richard M. Nixon. So proclaimed this poster during the investigation of political corruption in the early 1970s. The reports of investigative journalists led to jail time for many – and the President's resignation.

Introduction

I was 14 years old in June of 1972 when police arrested five men breaking into the Watergate headquarters of the Democratic Party. "I bet there's more to that story," commented my mother after reading a simple account of the burglary in the *Washington Post.* At least two members of the news media shared her intuition and curiosity: *Post* reporters Bob Woodward and Carl Bernstein. The commitment these journalists brought to uncovering the full story behind the Watergate break-in proved crucial to the nation's history. An incident that could have been dismissed as a third-rate burglary led instead to some of the most important news of the 20th century.

I grew up reading the unfolding reports of Woodward and Bernstein. While many of my peers paged through *Mad Magazine,* I studied the *Washington Post.* While other teens viewed reruns of *Gilligan's Island,* I watched live broadcasts of the U.S. Senate Watergate hearings. Overtime reporters and senators—with the support of the federal courts—traced the source of the burglary and its cover-up to the President of the United States: Richard M. Nixon. This dramatic revelation led to banner headlines in the *Washington Post* and other newspapers on August 9, 1974. "Nixon Resigns," screamed two-inch-tall letters on the only day in the nation's history when a U.S. President walked away from an uncompleted term of office.

My lifelong interest in politics emerged during this evolving tussle between the three branches of government: Congress, the courts, and the Presidency. At the same time I gained appreciation for a group that has sometimes been dubbed the unofficial fourth branch of our government: the news media. Journalists, as they did during Watergate, often serve as one more balancing power beyond the trio of legislative, judicial, and executive leadership. Their independence from government control gives them the freedom to investigate, exposé, and urge reform. At their best, journalists give voice to the concerns of the nation's citizens, and they call for the correction of the nation's faults. Journalists push the country's leaders to be more honest and fair.

Reporters like Woodward and Bernstein represent a storied tradition of in-depth news research and writing. The practice had its start in the 19th century, came to full bloom at the beginning of the 20th century, and continues to be used today. This book is about journalists who stepped forward 100 years ago to help rebalance the nation and its governance during an earlier era of disequilibrium. They wrote at a time when the nation's wealthiest citizens had gained exceptional power—yet its poorest citizens faced incredible hardship. They wrote when business and industry were expanding from local bases into national corporations—yet few laws existed to guide the effects of such growth. They wrote when political power often reflected the special interests of a small percentage of Americans—yet the voices and needs of the nation's majority went unheard and unmet.

The contradictions and challenges of 100 years ago echo through our own new century, too. At that time the transition was from a local and state perspective to a national one. Now we're transitioning from a national and continental view to one that circles the globe. International laws and practices are still emerging to guide that shift, much as federal legislation struggled to keep pace with growth at the beginning of the 20th century. Yet our changing outlook is accompanied by many of the same challenges that were faced 100 years ago: extreme wealth adjacent to extreme poverty, the corruption of the political process by influence and money, extraordinary profits within certain industries, and concerns about consumer safety.

"The journalist is a true servant of democracy. The best journalist of today occupies the exact place of the prophets of old: he cries out the truth and calls for reforms."
RAY STANNARD BAKER, DIARY ENTRY, CIRCA 1906

These parallels add to the relevance and meaning of the struggles from the beginning of the previous century. From 1903 to 1912 writers such as Lincoln Steffens exposéd how political corruption had become the "shame of the cities" and the "shame of the states." Ida Tarbell dug into corporate greed and the history of the Standard Oil Company until her investigative reports tarnished the reputations of the company and a founder—John D. Rockefeller, Sr. Upton Sinclair employed the tools of fiction in *The Jungle* to present the facts of worker exploitation in the greedy and unsavory world of Chicago meatpacking. Their colleagues wrote dozens of related stories about corruption and wrongdoing at the same time.

In 1906, after four years of such efforts, President Theodore Roosevelt suggested that at least some of these writers had crossed the line of decency, perhaps even truth (which they had not). He proposed that it wouldn't hurt for journalists to lighten up a bit from their raking up of muck, dirt, wrongdoing, and scandal. The term "muckrakers" and its uncomplimentary tone stuck. But the work did not stop.

Periods of muckraking have peppered our nation's history ever since. Often it is journalists and other writers—not lawyers, government officials, or politicians—who step forward during those crucial moments when the country wobbles out of balance. Investigative journalists—not lawyers—exposéd Senator Joseph McCarthy as a misguided anti-Communist in the 1950s. Investigative journalists—not government officials—revealed the hazardous, suppressed connection between cigarettes and cancer. Investigative journalists—not politicians—uncovered the scope of secretive surveillance and torture during the modern age of terrorism. These writers built upon the examples of courage and influence established by muckrakers a century ago. That enduring muckraking tradition—the commitment to get to the bottom of a story—will likely add a fourth branch of balance to the nation's governance for generations to come, as well.

This book is about the power of language. It is about the quest by news writers to uncover the truth, not just report surface facts. It is about having the vision—and patience—to study a clouded picture until the full view comes into focus. This book is about words so well researched and persuasively composed that they dismantle corporate monopolies, inspire political reforms, and modernize a way of life. It is about writers who capture the attention of a nation so that readers—even teenagers—hang on to every word. It is about words that change a nation.

Chapter 1

THE SHAME OF THE NATION

Lincoln Steffens had barely joined the editorial staff of **McClure's Magazine** before his energetic boss shooed him out the door of their New York offices. "Get out," commanded Samuel Sidney McClure. "Go anywhere, everywhere," he urged. "See what is going on in the cities and states, find out [what] we ought to be reporting." Taking his publisher at his word, Steffens hopped a train and followed his newsman's nose west. Soon he picked up the unmistakable stench of government corruption and tracked the smell to St. Louis, Missouri. Following up on a lead, he introduced himself to the area's recently elected circuit attorney, Joseph Folk.

Steffens found Folk locked in legal combat with a professional scoundrel—one of those unelected, behind-the-scenes, profit-driven manipulators of city government who were known at the turn of the last century as political bosses. Boss Ed Butler's influence was so widespread and his reach so strong that Folk seemed to fear for his safety. The prosecuting attorney kept looking over his shoulder "as if pursued" during his first meeting with Steffens, the newsman later recalled.

Folk claimed his stories of government corruption were "beyond belief." Seemingly every vote at the city council was managed by Butler, and bribery determined every outcome. Everything from street improvements to public transportation to government printing carried a hidden price. Butler promised "yes" votes by the city's elected assemblymen for one price; "no" votes sold for another.

Elected officials, bankers, merchants, even general citizens seemed to accept this political corruption as the cost of doing business in their city at the turn of the 20th century. Old-fashioned values like hard work and honesty appeared quaint, even expendable, in the face of fast-paced modern life. In the new century, the lure and power of money—greed—reigned supreme. In St. Louis millions of dollars exchanged hands in bribes and counterbribes so that business leaders could modernize and prosper. This amount of money was significant even then; today it would be the equivalent of hundreds of millions of dollars.

Investigative reports filled the pages of McClure's within a year of the first Shame of the Cities article by Lincoln Steffens. Steffens and staff writers such as Ida M. Tarbell and Ray

Stannard Baker researched each story exhaustively.

Steffens had unearthed his story. He was outraged by the scale of the abuses taking place in St. Louis and inspired by Folk's determination to fight back. He hoped readers would share his own anger and would cheer for a victory by the prosecutor. Steffens hired a local news reporter to research and write up the details of the story for the magazine. Then he headed back to New York.

When the story caught up with him back at his office, Steffens observed that the freelancer had "left out some salient facts ... [and] 'gone easy' on the boss, Ed Butler." When Steffens restored the missing facts, the local reporter panicked. He told Steffens that "he could not live and work in St. Louis if the article was printed as I had edited it." He insisted Steffens "sign it with him and take the blame" for the changes. Thus this story bore a shared byline when it ran in the October 1902 issue of *McClure's*.

Bribery and corruption often accompanied the growth of public transportation (above, streetcars in St. Louis, Mo., in 1890).

Steffens took off his editor's hat and, from then on, took up full-time reporting; he and McClure realized now that only a visiting reporter could get away with unflinching exposés of local problems. They understood, too, that their story about St. Louis was but one example of a repeating American pattern. Corruption had crept into cities and states throughout the country.

After Steffens published a follow-up piece entitled "The Shame of Minneapolis," letters began flooding the magazine's office with other stories of hometown abuse. "Evidently you could shoot me out of a gun fired at random," Steffens observed to his publisher, "and wherever I lighted, there would be a story, the same way." McClure preferred the more scientific (and profitable) approach of selecting well-populated cities that featured dramatic tales of trouble and triumph. He hoped to capture new readers as well as news.

First Steffens returned to St. Louis for an update on Folk's battle against "The Shamelessness of St. Louis." Stories followed about tainted politics in Pittsburgh and corrupt leadership in Philadelphia. He reported on reform efforts by honest officials to undo a history of corruption in Chicago and on how New York City was putting "Good Government to the Test." In 1904 McClure published a collection of the seven articles by Steffens, titled *The Shame of the Cities.* By then Steffens was already working on a companion series looking at state political corruption.

Such extensive travel and research was not cheap. By McClure's calculations, he invested some $3,000 in each report, or more than $40,000 apiece in today's currency. McClure recouped his investments when the stories attracted new subscribers to the magazine. Reader response determined whether or not a series would continue. "No response—no more chapters," recalled one writer. "A healthy response—as many chapters as the material justified." More readers, in turn, meant more advertisers. A growing variety of products were now available nationally, and businesses were eager to market their wares to all these potential new customers.

Abraham Lincoln, from whom Steffens had earned his first name, spoke during the Civil War about fighting so that "government of the people, by the people, for the people, shall not perish from the earth." Like most Americans, Steffens had grown up believing that the nation's governments worked with textbook simplicity and virtue. When he found exactly the opposite to be true, he used his own shock to likewise alarm his readers. Steffens hoped his reports would spark the nation to fulfill the potential envisioned by Lincoln, instead of being a "government of the people, by the rascals, for the rich."

"If I should be entrusted with the work I think I could make my name."
—LINCOLN STEFFENS, 1902
WRITING TO THE STAFF AT *MCCLURE'S* AFTER RESEARCHING A SERIES ON CITY GOVERNMENT

His articles did just that. Steffens's study of the shame of U.S. cities and states amounted to a shame of the nation. His stories showed that problems occurring in one community were being repeated elsewhere. His writings, and articles by others, generated alarm and prompted calls for action.

Citizens elected reform-minded leaders and removed corrupt officials from office. They called for an end to backroom deals and for more government control over citywide services, such as streetcar lines, garbage collection, and the public water supply. Successes in one city inspired similar reforms in others. And while reform didn't remove all corruption, it did help cleanup local and state governments. Regional improvements set the stage for subsequent calls for greater honesty in the national government, as well.

The voice of Lincoln Steffens was joined by a chorus of other writers at *McClure's* and elsewhere who exposéd corruption and called for improvements at the beginning of the 20th century. They called themselves reform journalists, national journalists, or authors of the literature of exposure. President Theodore Roosevelt labeled their efforts torrential journalism because it contained so much evidence and prompted such indignation. Not until 1906, when this chorus of reform-minded publishing had reached a roar, would the President propose a new name for these writers: muckrakers.

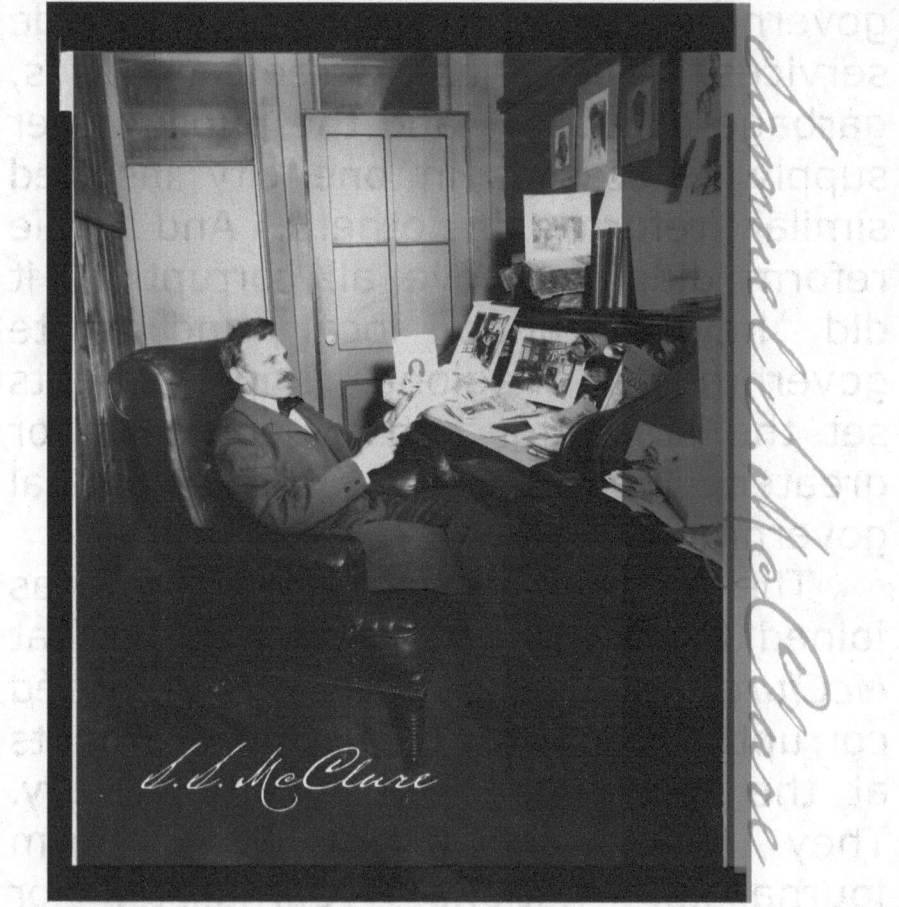

Chapter 2

MUCKRAKER ORIGINS

Neither Lincoln Steffens nor any of his colleagues at the beginning of the 20th century can claim to be the first muckrakers. Newspapers and magazines have alerted readers about corruption and wrongdoing almost from their earliest years of publication. By the closing decades of the 1800s, though, more and more reporters were researching and writing investigative news stories. Nellie Bly checked herself into a mental institution to gather facts for an exposé about the mistreatment of the mentally ill. Danish immigrant Jacob Riis increased awareness about the inhuman conditions shared by the urban poor through his writing and photography. African-American journalist Ida B. Wells-Barnett documented the scope and horrors of the lynching of blacks in the United States. All three writers did more than share unsettling news. They prompted citizens to fight for reform.

Muckraking is sometimes confused with yellow journalism, a genre that developed during the second half of the 19th century. Both forms of reporting commanded public attention with shocking news. But the two styles differed in one key way: Muckraking depended on facts. Yellow journalism exaggerated. Its stories focused on grisly, crime-based news and other sensational headlines that sold papers. This style of reporting gained its colorful name because many of these papers published the "Yellow Kid" comic strip with a yellow-inked main character. Today's supermarket tabloids publish in the tradition of yellow journalism.

In 1893, when S.S. McClure's namesake magazine hit the news-stands for the first time, he joined the swelling ranks of nationally distributed magazines. These periodicals combined the latest fiction and poetry with reports of scientific discoveries, popular history, and current events. McClure brought an infectious level of irrepressible energy and enthusiasm to his work. He traveled and read widely, always on the lookout for new story ideas and promising writers. At the end of every trip he would rush to the sixth-floor offices of *McClure's* in lower Manhattan. Grinning broadly "with his valise full of clippings, papers, books, and letters," he would bubble over with ideas, enthusiasm, and marching orders. "He was all intuition and impulse, bursting with nervous energy," recalled one of his writers.

Jacob Riis, a Danish immigrant and respected journalist, denounced the poverty and exploitation of the urban poor in his 1890 book, How the Other Half Lives. The book's illustrations were based on photographs by the author. As part of this documentation, Riis photographed children sleeping on the streets of New York City (above). Lincoln Steffens collaborated with this early muckraker during shared days as newspaper reporters.

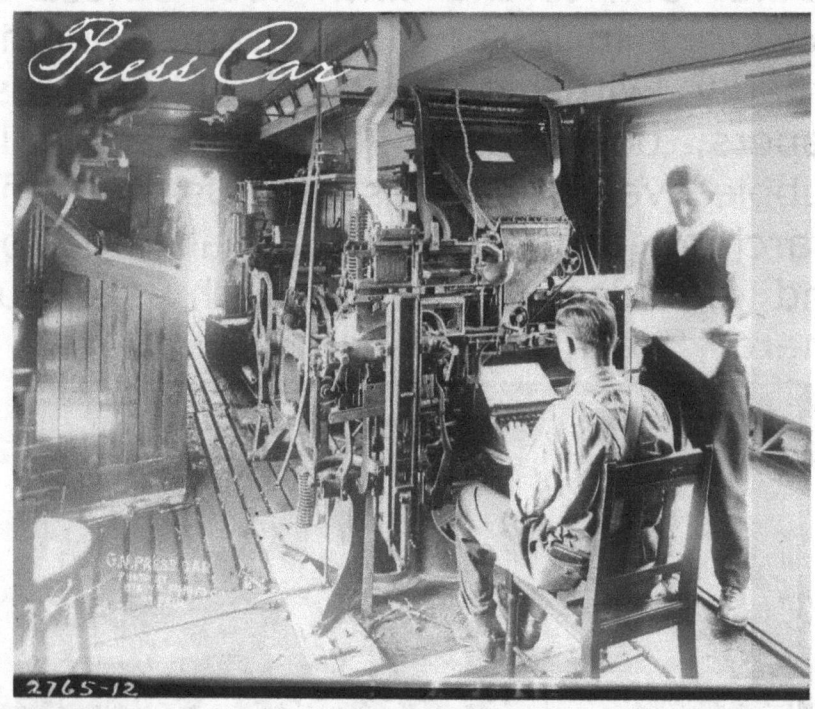

Reporters followed the newsmakers at the turn of the last century, just as they do today. Railroad press cars served as the equivalent of today's TV broadcast vans with satellite disks. Reporters could write, typeset (above), and even print their stories as trains carrying dignitaries moved from place to place. Such innovations helped make news more timely and encouraged public interest in current events.

A series of events at the turn of the century helped push *McClure's* and other publications toward the journalism that would become known as muckraking. The first was the Spanish-American War of 1898, a struggle over Spain's colonial presence in nearby Cuba and other territories. The assassination of William McKinley in 1901 by an antigovernment anarchist was another. The assumption of the Presidency by reform-minded Theodore Roosevelt served as a third.

Each event reminded citizens that the world was becoming more complicated, and each one aroused the public's curiosity and emotion. Journalists stepped in to satisfy the growing public interest in current events and to explain how the nation fitted within an increasingly complex world. Magazines were particularly well suited to meet the needs of modern readers; their weekly or monthly publication schedules permitted more time for story development, research, and analysis. The restrictions of a daily newspaper cycle did not apply.

In addition to these more distant political events, citizens faced unprecedented changes closer to home. Gone were the days when farming dominated the nation's economy. Business, transportation, and manufacturing ruled the day. Cities expanded in size and influence. Swelling numbers of immigrants competed for jobs and resources. Individual workers joined together in labor unions to bargain for better working conditions and strike if they did not get them. Mechanization brought new conveniences but altered old ways of life. The stability of the family shook: Young people delayed or avoided marriage, and divorce rates increased. Organized vices—from drinking at saloons to prostitution in brothels—tested the nation's morality.

A few thousand turn-of-the-century millionaires controlled nine-tenths of the nation's resources. They set the pace for its policies, influenced the work of its elected officials, and determined the working conditions for the majority of the country's 76 million residents. With few exceptions, they happily ignored the hardships suffered by the workers who contributed to their wealth. Middle-class citizens found themselves sandwiched between the excessive wealth of a few people and the vast needs of many.

This heartless attitude contrasted with values linked to the nation's religious heritage. Generations had grownup learning the so-called Golden Rule: Do unto others as you would have them do unto you. Even those with limited access to books usually had read *The Pilgrim's Progress,* by John Bunyan, an allegorical tale of the triumph of goodness over evil. As education became more available to men and women alike, people began to question the contradictions taking place around them. Was the nation losing sight of the Golden Rule? Gould society modernize and still stay fair?

Science helped fuel the muckraker movement, too. Although some citizens rejected the theory of natural selection set forth by Charles Darwin, others embraced it as a model for improvement. Couldn't society evolve—in the same way as animals and plants—by favoring its better traits over its worst? Could the techniques employed in science and exploration be used to discover better ways to improve the world? Even as science offered new models for asking questions, religion provided a comforting reminder of human virtues such as love, sacrifice, brotherhood, and kindness. The two fields combined into an inspiring blend of modern wonder and ancient wisdom.

History provided a final influence. Adults in 1900 had grown up in the shadow of the Civil War. Abraham Lincoln's assassination served as the first political memory for a generation. Lincoln Steffens literally bore the martyred President's name. Citizens seemed to feel almost duty-bound to fulfill President Lincoln's unfinished vision of creating a nation of, by, and for the people. (One hundred years later the assassination of another President—John F. Kennedy—would likewise prompt a generation to act in a leader's memory.)

> "When Mr. Steffens, Mr. Baker, Miss Tarbell write, they must never be conscious of anything else ... other than telling an absorbing story: the story is thing."
> S.S. MCCLURE, 1905
> EXPLAINING THE PUBLISHING

PHILOSOPHY OF MCCLURE'S MAGAZINE

"I can't sit still," S.S. McClure once told his staff. "That's your job." McClure preferred to travel and look for story ideas – especially in Europe. He Tallied 149 trips across the Atlantic, often in the company of his wife.

All these factors inspired what came to be known as the Progressive era. Progressives thought that by working together they could make genuine improvements—progress—in the lifestyle and governance of the modern world. In this dynamic environment, *McClure's* could "no longer be content with being merely attractive, readable," one of its writers later explained. "It was a citizen and wanted to do a citizen's part." Readers hungered for probing stories that shocked and challenged them. As a result, not only did investigative reporting suit the times politically, it made good business sense, too.

McClure was among the first to notice a shift in writer and reader interest, beginning with the January 1903 edition of his magazine. At first this issue seemed like any other number of *McClure's Magazine:* five short stories, six news articles, a handful of poems. Then the staff began to notice "a coincidence that ... set us thinking." McClure dashed off a quick editorial. He observed how the magazine contained three articles on the same subject: the "American Contempt of Law." Each story reported on behavior that was dishonorable at best, illegal at worst. "Capitalists, workingmen, politicians, citizens—all breaking the law or letting it be broken. Who is left to uphold it?" McClure asked. His answer: "There is none left but all of us."

Each of the three articles presented a wealth of facts and an undertone of outrage. The first piece was "The Shame of Minneapolis" by Lincoln Steffens. Ida M. Tarbell, an accomplished biographer and journalist, authored another. Her work represented the continuation of a series she and McClure had started two months earlier about John D. Rockefeller, Sr., and the history of the Standard Oil Company. The third news story, an article by Ray Stannard Baker, examined tensions between labor unions, nonunionized workers, and employers.

The beginning of a movement can be hard to pinpoint. As far as investigative journalism is concerned, though, it was at this moment that what would later become known as muckraking took form. These three stories were not the first such pieces, and three years would pass before this style of hard-hitting, in-depth, exhaustively researched reporting would earn its controversial name. But by identifying the theme of lawlessness—of dishonorable, even dishonest, behavior—and calling on citizens to reform it, McClure and *McClure's Magazine* helped launch a movement.

Unlike most publishers, McClure paid his reporters a salary. Newspapers and magazines traditionally paid news writers a set fee based on how many words or column inches of type were published. By paying his authors a monthly salary, McClure freed them to spend weeks, even years, researching and writing a story. McClure expected his well-paid writers to meet demanding standards. Every article had to be thoroughly researched, buttressed with facts, and analyzed scientifically. Yet the writing had to be engaging. Articles might be written, edited, and rewritten multiple times before publication. McClure wanted objective content about shocking topics. He might use sensational headlines to attract readers, but the copy itself was balanced in tone. Readers were left to draw their own conclusions.

In 1922, some ten years after the muckraking era's demise, Ray Stannard Baker recalled how outraged a reader had been that Baker had not condemned the villains in one of his muckraking stories. "If I got mad, you wouldn't," Baker replied to the reader. "I always had the feeling," observed Baker, "that if I let off steam in my articles the reader himself would feel quite relieved and never want to do anything."

McClure, like Baker, did not want to let readers off the hook. He saw ordinary people and their capacity to demand change as the best cure for whatever ailed the United States. "If we let in light and air, if the people understand," he observed in the magazine a few years later, then readers may be encouraged to "at least proceed forward." McClure hoped his magazine and its troop of capable writers would inspire a social revolution.

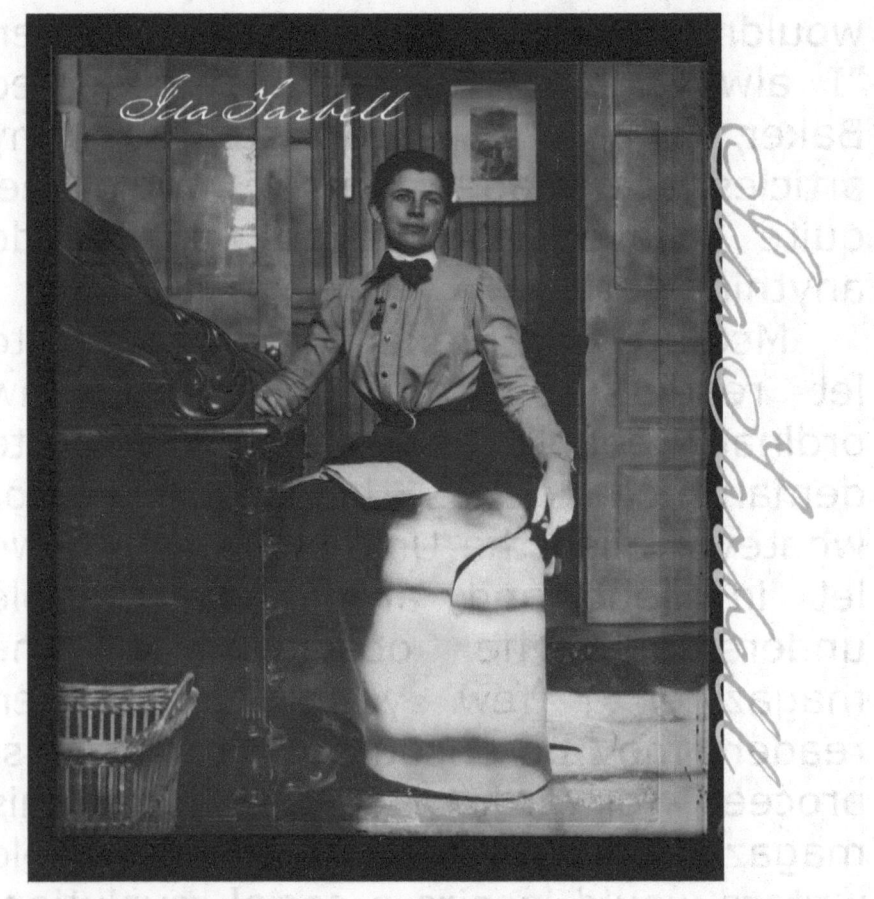

Chapter 3

FIGHTING THE OCTOPUS

In the rapid-firing, bustling mind of S.S. McClure, Ida Tarbell was the perfect reporter to tackle an investigation of John D. Rockefeller, Sr., and the Standard Oil Company. In addition to her skills as a researcher and author, Tarbell practically had oil running through her veins. In August 1859, when she was just 21 months old, her father, Franklin Sumner Tarbell, had found himself in the right place at the right time during the birth of the oil industry. That month, not far from the family home in Titusville, Pennsylvania, an enterprising speculator drilled the world's first oil well. Tarbell, a carpenter by trade, seized the opportunity to solve the chief problem caused by pumping quantities of oil out of the ground: Where does one put it? With Tarbell's Tank Shops he created a quick and profitable solution by building wooden tanks that could store as much as 100 barrels of oil at a time.

Always inquisitive, young Ida Tarbell (above, with a newspaper) wanted to become a scientist. In 1876 she enrolled at nearby Allegheny College, the only woman in a class with 40 men. After graduating, she used her investigative skills as a reporter instead.

The discovery of oil in western Pennsylvania brought the usual boom-and-bust swings of speculation. The region witnessed a rush to drill more wells, followed by oversupply, then scarcity as wells went dry. This environment fostered cutthroat competition and attracted the attention of a little-known investor named John D. Rockefeller. An enterprising wholesaler in Ohio, he fell into the oil refining business almost by accident in 1863. Seven years later, with his interests growing larger and stronger, Rockefeller and two partners incorporated their holdings into the Standard Oil Company. They then proceeded to expand their business exponentially by squeezing small-time operators and independent contractors out of the market—including men like Franklin Tarbell.

The tentacles of "the octopus," as Standard Oil would later be called, advanced with stealth in these early years—and lightning efficiency. Company officials secretly negotiated favorable shipping rates for moving oil by railroad. They bullied small suppliers of oil and pressured them to sell their operations. Within two decades, what started as just another oil company had mushroomed into a monumental monopoly—the Standard Oil Trust. The octopus became so powerful and feared that, when Franklin Tarbell learned his daughter planned to write about Standard Oil, he exclaimed: "Don't do it, Ida—they will ruin the magazine."

Unfazed by her father's warning, Tarbell plunged into the task. She started work in the fall of 1901. (That same season Theodore Roosevelt settled into the role of U.S. President.) During her multi-state investigation, she battled mistrust, secrecy, cold trails, and the many tentacles that stretched from Standard Oil. For more than a year, Tarbell tracked down hot tips, reviewed public documents, and interviewed old-timers from the oil rush. She questioned sources at Standard Oil and related businesses, keeping comments off the record when contacts insisted on remaining anonymous.

As a youth, Tarbell had enjoyed looking at things under a microscope. Now she practiced that patient skill in her systematic scrutiny of Rockefeller and Standard Oil. When it came time to write, Tarbell's lifelong habit of making lists and outlines helped her organize the "appalling heaps of documentary stuff" she had collected.

A simple series of three articles mushroomed over time into plans for 6, then 12, and finally some 20 pieces. The first story, "The Birth of an Industry," ran in the November 1902 issue of *McClure's*. Eight monthly installments followed. Readers were horrified to learn that the company had reached its impressive size thanks to greed-driven, ruthless business practices.

Forests of oil derricks replaced whole hillsides of trees in western Pennsylvania in the decades that followed the development there of the oil industry. Tarbell lived near these oil-pumping structures for about half of her childhood.

"Next!" With an oil tank representing its body, the Standard Oil octopus extends a free arm toward the White House in this 1904 cartoon. Other tentacles already control state and federal capitols, shipyards, railroads, and executives at steel and copper companies.

Standard Oil had used every dirty trick in the book—and invented some new ones—in order to attain its mammoth size. The company had made secret bookkeeping records, conspired with railroad executives, bribed officials, threatened its competitors, and sabotaged the property of its rivals as it worked to gain the upper hand in the oil business. In the process people like Rockefeller had become multimillionaires. Tarbell's revelations of intrigue and cutthroat competition fascinated the general public. Readers clamored for more articles, McClure extended the series, and Tarbell renewed her research.

In the end Tarbell put three intense years into the research and writing of what became known as *The History of the Standard Oil Company.* McClure, honoring his commitment to pay on salary instead of by the word, invested an estimated $4,000 into each article of the series, for a total of some $80,000. In addition to Tarbell's salary and research expenses, McClure covered the costs of a part-time research assistant based, like Standard Oil, in Cleveland, Ohio. A climax of Tarbell's sleuthing; came in October 1903, when she, her assistant, and a sketch artist surreptitiously attended a church where Rockefeller was service in Cleveland scheduled to speak. "It was worth the trip," Tarbell recorded in her unedited notes. This view of Rockefeller would be her closest encounter with the oil tycoon: All her requests for interviews were denied.

> "[Standard Oil] had never played fair, and that ruined their greatness for me."
> —IDA TARBELL, 1939
> WRITING IN HER AUTOBIOGRAPHY ABOUT THE STANDARD OIL COMPANY

Part two of Tarbell's series debuted in December 1903. As before, she wrote "in the dispassionate manner associated with *McClure's,*" observes Rockefeller biographer Ron Ghernow. However, her text "was always informed by indignation that throbbed just below the surface," he notes. "By writing in such a relatively cool style, she made her readers boil with anger." Tarbell seethed about the examples of greed and corruption she found during her research. No doubt she sympathized with the independent operators—including family members and friends—who had lost their livelihood during the expansion of Standard Oil.

Tarbell's conclusion to the series hit the newsstands in October 1904. During the course of her reports, the magazine's circulation had grown by 100,000 to reach almost the half-million mark. Her completed series was published immediately as a two-volume book. Soon after, Tarbell wrote an in-depth character sketch on Rockefeller that appeared in *McClure's* during the summer of 1905.

Contrary to the warnings of Tarbell's father, the octopus did not ruin *McClure's Magazine*. Company officials elected not to challenge Tarbell's reports. Perhaps they felt that rebutting her few mistakes would only emphasize the truth of the rest of her charges. "Not a word. Not a word about that misguided woman," Rockefeller is said to have told a mutual friend. "It has always been the policy of the Standard to keep silent under attack and let their acts speak for themselves," he told another.

John D. Rockefeller, Sr. (above, in 1905), remained unruffled in public Ida Tarbell's reports for McClure's, but in private his health suffered. His wife and grown children developed depression and other ailments from the strain.

In this case silence spoke volumes. Biographer Chernow claims that Tarbell's work "turned America's most private man into its most public and hated figure." The Rockefeller family brought in their own writers and advisers to help erase the damage done by her series. These early public relations consultants suggested story ideas to newspapers and played up the human side of the oil magnate—his love of golf, for instance. Rockefeller, although already involved in philanthropy, began giving away even more of his money. Critics charged that he was trying to buy an improved reputation. Many decades would pass before his value as a benefactor would eclipse the negative view of him as a business executive.

Tarbell's exposé intensified federal scrutiny of Standard Oil, as well. The company owed much of its success to its clever exploitation of contradictory state laws during an era of limited federal government. The United States were like "40 or 50 odd little republics," observed McClure. Standard Oil avoided regulations and scrutiny in one state by setting up operations in another state where no such laws or oversight existed.

President Roosevelt—aided by the embarrassing publicity of the muckrakers—pushed for greater federal authority through new national laws. He created a Department of Commerce and Labor to help with enforcement. The department's Bureau of Corporations had the authority to investigate the nation's businesses, and it did just that with Standard Oil. One suit led to the "big fine" penalty of $29 million against the octopus for its scheme to set favorable rates with the railroads. Later on, however, this fine was judged excessive and the conviction overturned by a federal appeals court.

A separate case approached Standard Oil from a different tack. It used the Sherman Antitrust Act of 1890—one of the first federal laws to address big business—to argue that Standard Oil had grown into a monopoly by squeezing out competition. The case led to a 1909 verdict against the company that was upheld by the Supreme Court in 1911. The courts ordered Standard Oil to sell off many of its holdings, although a core of the original company could remain intact. Ironically, those very sales made

Rockefeller the richest man in the world, almost a billionaire.

Whatever laws Rockefeller and the octopus may have broken, Tarbell judged by an even higher standard, one that reflected the religious background of the era. "I accuse Mr. Rockefeller not of breaking the law or even the rules of business," observed Tarbell. "I judge him by the golden rule." Rockefeller had made ruthless greed a key component of his business plan. Neither Tarbell nor other mainstream American citizens found anything to admire about that.

Chapter 4

LABOR AND LAMB CHOPS

Upton Sinclair, unlike Ida Tarbell and Lincoln Steffens, freelanced with his pen. As one writing job ended, he hunted up the next. In the fall of 1904, when a Midwestern weekly invited him to write a series of articles about the hardships of factory work, Sinclair jumped at the chance. He knew firsthand about the challenges faced by day laborers living on the edge of poverty. Sinclair had grown up moving from place to place with his parents—living well sometimes and impoverished at others—depending upon the reliability and health of his alcoholic father.

As a freelance writer, the adult Sinclair often found himself underpaid and underfed, too. He wanted to show how the wealth of American business owners came at the expense of its workers. Long hours, grueling conditions, and low wages diminished the lives of working-class citizens. These people toiled on holidays, often even on Christmas, and received no vacation time or sick pay. Frequently they worked extra hours without the benefit of overtime pay. They received no health insurance or pension. Compensation for work-related injury—even death or the loss of limbs—was inadequate, if it existed at all.

Sinclair hoped to provoke outrage among readers over these abuses and spark wider citizen support for an increasingly popular idea about how to organize business: socialism. If all the people of the society owned the nation's factories and services—instead of just a few wealthy citizens—surely greater fairness would follow. Just 26 years old, Sinclair plunged into his assignment. He and his editor at *the Appeal to Reason* chose Chicago and its meatpacking industry as the setting for his study.

That fall he began visiting the city's packinghouses, even as Tarbell concluded *The History of the Standard Oil Company*, as Steffens explored "The

Shame of the States," and as Ray Stannard Baker and other writers at *McClure's* and elsewhere persisted in exposing the "American Contempt of Law." No one had yet thought to label these champions of social justice as muckrakers, and readers remained keenly interested in their reports.

The animal noise of the Chicago stockyards equaled "all the barnyards of the universe," wrote Upton Sinclair. Forget counting the animals: "it would have taken all day simply to count the pens." Thousands of animals could walk off railroad cars one day, then be butchered and packed off as sausages and cuts of meat the next.

Upton Sinclair disguised the names of Chicago meatpackers in his articles as Anderson, Smith, and Morton. When The Jungle appeared in book form, the big three became Durham, Brown, and Jones.

Three meatpacking firms—Armour, Swift, and Morris—dominated the business of Packingtown, as Chicago's stockyards were called. Livestock arrived via railway cars, then entered the sprawling acres of paddocks assigned to cattle, hogs, and sheep. After being purchased, animals were herded through chutes toward modern slaughterhouses. Decades before Henry Ford ostensibly invented the assembly line in his automobile factory, meatpackers—by breaking what was once a specialized craft into a sequence of isolated tasks—beat him to the idea, albeit it as a disassembly line. Each slaughterhouse worker earned a descriptive job title and then repeated the same task over and over, ten or more hours a day, six days a week.

   Animals that stepped onto the killing floors were promptly dispatched by knockers. Next, stickers slit the throats of dead and dying animals attached to mechanical lifts. These hoists carried the carcasses past a sequence of workstations where skinners, boners, and trimmers would quarter and carve the beasts. Luggers hauled slabs of meat into refrigerated rooms and railway cars. This same division of labor occurred at on-site smokehouses, canning rooms, and sausage works.

Sinclair stepped into the world of Packingtown dressed in his worn-out clothes, carrying a lunch pail. By blending in with thousands of other workers, he slipped in and out of packinghouses for a firsthand look at working conditions. To avoid suspicion, he kept track in his head of what he saw and then made notes about it later on. He visited the factories over and over until he had recorded sufficient detail.

Sinclair slept and ate at a nearby settlement house, an early version of a social services center. He met with its Packingtown residents, interviewing laborers, family members, the unemployed, the injured and maimed. He talked to social workers. He even compared notes with a British journalist who was in town conducting his own study of meatpacking sanitation. Recalling his research decades later in his autobiography, Sinclair noted: "I went about white-faced and thin, partly from undernourishment, partly from horror" at what he observed.

After seven weeks of research, Sinclair felt armed with enough facts and stories of human anguish to inspire a social revolution. He began writing his series for the *Appeal* later that year. Sinclair chose to relay his information in the form of a novel, patterning it after the era's childhood favorite, *The Pilgrim's Progress*. In John Bunyan's 17th-century classic morality tale, the central character, Christian, travels through a lifetime's worth of temptations, trials, and woes, in order to reach at journey's end the gates of the Celestial City, or heaven.

Sinclair created the character Jurgis Rudkos, a Lithuanian immigrant, in the mold of Christian. Then he proceeded to test Jurgis and his family with all the challenges Sinclair had witnessed in Packingtown. Before the tale ends, his characters experience real estate fraud, poverty, child labor, immobilizing winter weather, frostbite, injury, loss of jobs, childbirth, death, blood poisoning, breathing disorders, poor sanitation, attacks by rats, temptation by alcohol, extortion, crime, jail, political corruption, homelessness, and prostitution.

Meatpackers boasted of how, with great economy, their enterprise used "everything about the pig except the squeal." Workers harvested hog bristles for brushes, sheep's wool for clothing, and animal gut fibers for violin strings.

Sinclair peppered his text with metaphors, equating Packingtown with a jungle and comparing its workers to cogs in a machine and to animals. He connected the fates of the slaughtered animals to those of the slaughterhouse workers. "Murder it was that went on there upon the killing-floor, systematic, deliberate and hideous murder," he wrote. "They were slaughtering men there, just as certainly as they were slaughtering cattle; they were grinding the bodies and souls of them, and turning them into dollars and cents." Sinclair's novel, like *The Pilgrim's Progress,* ended with salvation, but *The Jungle's* hero did not discover it by entering a Celestial City. Instead he joined the Socialist Party. The novel suggested that socialism could solve the problems of modern industry.

When the *Appeal* began publishing Sinclair's work in serial form the next spring, it seemed to hit its mark. Installments boosted sales of the *Appeal,* much as S.S. McClure's exposés had done for his magazine. By late 1905—as Sinclair prepared to transform his installments into a book—fellow author and socialist Jack London offered an exuberant endorsement. "Dear Comrades: Here it is at last!" he began. *The Jungle* "depicts what our country really is, the home of oppression and injustice, a nightmare of misery ... a jungle of wild beasts." London predicted that the book "will open countless ears that have been deaf to Socialism.... It will wake thousands of converts to our cause." Then he signed his endorsement, "Yours for the revolution, Jack London."

Not everyone shared such enthusiasm. Sinclair's first book publisher found the finished novel too horrifying to print. After Sinclair refused to revise its gory content, his publisher canceled their contract. Sinclair's second publisher sent investigators to quietly confirm key facts in the story before agreeing to produce the work. At the same time Sinclair revised his manuscript, shortening it by five chapters and deleting key details and metaphors. Controversy endures over which version of *The Jungle* is more genuine—its serial form or the book edition. Both are in print today.

The Jungle hit bookstores in February 1906, and became an immediate best seller, both in the United States and abroad. To Sinclair's dismay, however, the subject that captivated readers of his book was not the working conditions endured by the slaughterhouse laborers. Readers focused instead on the quality of Packingtown meat products—food they put on their own tables.

Even as The Jungle reached the public (top, a book poster), other publications exposéd further meatpacking horrors.

Among the details Sinclair had used to bolster the authenticity of his work were examples of poor sanitation at the meatpacking facilities. Workers stood in pools of animal blood and entrails. Spoiled and condemned meat was added to the sausage grinders. Flies were everywhere. Rats ran about the place. Blended meat products called "deviled chicken" or "potted ham" might actually contain no trace of a chicken or hog. Rumors circulated that human body parts—even whole workers—had disappeared into meat recipes.

The public "took a book of well over 300 pages and concentrated on perhaps ten or 30 pages meant by the author to be true and effective, but hardly central," observed historian Robert M. Grunden years later. In doing so, most readers overlooked the pro-socialist thread Sinclair had woven so carefully throughout the book. Food safety caught their attention instead.

"Mary had a little lamb and when she saw it sicken she shipped it off to packingtown, and now it's labeled chicken."

—VERSE PUBLISHED IN THE *NEW YORK EVENING POST* IN RESPONSE TO *THE JUNGLE*

This topic had come to readers' attention even before publication of *The Jungle* thanks to the work of other reform journalists. These earlier stories had prompted President Theodore Roosevelt—who liked to be out front on reform issues—to call for action. In December of 1905, he urged Congress to enact a law "to regulate interstate commerce in misbranded and adulterated food, drinks, and drugs." The publication of *The Jungle* two months later added ammunition and public support to this call for reform.

Meatpackers, avoiding John D. Rockefeller's strategy of stony silence, insisted that Sinclair's allegations were false. Ogden Armour, without mentioning *The Jungle,* branded the work "yellow literature." Meatpackers pressured their allies in Congress to fight reform.

Meanwhile, Roosevelt ordered investigations of Sinclair's charges. He learned that the realities of Packingtown were, if anything, even more disgusting and vile than those presented in *The Jungle*. Roosevelt ratcheted up his pressure on Congress. With the public in an uproar as well, the legislators caved. On June 30, Roosevelt signed into law the Pure Food and Drug Act of 1906 and a related meat inspection amendment.

Sinclair had achieved reform. Instead of sparking the socialist revolution he had sought, however, his writing had prompted the middle class to insist upon safer food. As Sinclair observed later that year: "I aimed at the public's heart, and by accident I hit it in the stomach."

Chapter 5

SHAKING THE FOUNDATIONS

On April 18, 1906, a now-famed earthquake tumbled the foundations of San Francisco. Even as the city caught fire and burned, reform journalists were already digging out from the rubble created in their own world four days earlier during a speech by Theodore Roosevelt. The President's remarks reflected an unease that had grown within him for months. "Put sky in the landscape," he had urged S.S. McClure the previous fall. Roosevelt suggested that **McClure's** investigate crime at all levels of society, not just among the heights of big business. Although the President collaborated with Upton Sinclair following the publication some months later of *The Jungle,* he lost patience as the author badgered him to take action. Roosevelt, exasperated, sent a message to the author's publisher: "Tell Sinclair to go home and let me run the country for a while."

Then, in March 1906, *Cosmopolitan Magazine* began publishing a series about government corruption that pushed President Roosevelt over the edge. The reach of corporate influence leads all the way to the nation's capital, warned David Graham Phillips in his "Treason of the Senate" series. In the course of nine installments, the reporter systematically exposéd corporate links with U.S. senators from such far-flung states as New York, Missouri, Texas, West Virginia, and Wisconsin. Phillips questioned how legislators could earn thousands of dollars in fees for serving on the boards of directors for dozens of corporations and then step into the Senate chamber as if these connections would not influence their votes.

At that time senators earned their seats by appointment through state legislatures (according to rules established in the U.S. Constitution). Phillips argued that the very selection of senators was tainted through behind-the-scenes manipulation by business interests. Phillips named names and pulled no punches in his revelations about Senate corruption. Quoting the U.S. Constitution's definition of treason, he characterized senators as a band of corrupt officials "giving aid and comfort" to the enemies of the people: the self-serving owners of big business. (His charges echo today's concern that corporate and special interest groups could influence legislators by contributing funds to their political campaigns.)

Sales of Cosmopolitan Magazine soared with the "Treason of the Senate" series by David Graham Phillips. The author urged readers to "judge public men by what they do and are, not by what they say and pretend."

"Patent medicines are poisoning people throughout America today," proclaimed a Collier's story about the sale of alcohol- and chemical-laced remedies.

Roosevelt fumed. As much as he knew that truth lay behind many of Phillips's claims, this series hit close to home, perhaps too close. The stories leveled charges at men whom the President counted as Republican Party allies, personal friends, and political associates. Many had stood behind his successful election to the Presidency in 1904. Roosevelt may have worried that the public would assume that he, too, could be bought by special interests.

The President seized the opportunity to rebut Phillips's allegations at an off-the-record speech to members of a local club of reporters. Satisfied with this private hearing, he repeated the lengthy speech on April 14, 1906, at a cornerstone-laying ceremony for a new House office building. On each occasion the President evoked parallels between current events and a passage from that favorite book of childhood reading—not just of reform journalists but of his audience and the nation in general—*The Pilgrim's Progress,* by John Bunyan.

"In *Pilgrim's Progress* the Man with the Muckrake is set forth as an example of him whose vision is fixed on carnal instead of spiritual things," Roosevelt reminded his listeners. "Yet he also typifies the man who in this life consistently refuses to see aught that is lofty, and fixes his eyes with solemn intentness only on that which is vile and debasing."

To Roosevelt, reform journalists (muckrakers) had become so obsessed with their quest for exposé (muck) that they had forgotten to examine the goodness around them (as symbolized by a celestial crown held, unobserved, above the muckrakers head in Bunyan's novel). "The man who never does anything else, who never thinks or speaks or writes save of his feats with the muckrake, speedily becomes, not a help to society, not an incitement to good, but one of the most potent forces of evil."

Roosevelt went on to suggest that exaggerated claims led listeners to become cynical, to "grow as suspicious of the accusation as of the offense," and thus lose their ability to be aroused later on by truthful charges. He advised advocates to investigate the evils that flourished among the "have-nots," too, not just the wealthy "man of capital." Perhaps thinking of Sinclair and his calls for socialism, Roosevelt warned that "the wild preachers of unrest and discontent, the wild agitators against the entire existing order, ... all these men are the most dangerous opponents of real reform."

Although Roosevelt praised individuals "who with stern sobriety and truth assail the many evils of our times," the damage was done. "Well, you've put an end to all these journalistic investigations that have made you," Lincoln Steffens told the President the day after his speech.

Roosevelt protested to Steffens that he had done no such thing, but in truth he had dealt the genre a crippling blow. Now the "progressive President ... had called reform journalists extremist, and any further exposures could be dismissed as mere 'muckraking,'" explains historian Robert M. Crunden. (In subsequent eras, politicians have used labels such as "soft on communism" and "unpatriotic" to stifle debate in the same dismissive way.) Perhaps Roosevelt felt secretly pleased at the effects of his remarks. He remained the reform President, free to run—and expand—the federal government in a way that looked out for the people. If calls were needed for further reform, Roosevelt may have reasoned, they could be raised by the era's diverse collection of political parties.

President Theodore Roosevelt cleans up the muck of Senate corruption single-handedly in this cartoon. Journalists are left out of the picture.

Ironically, as Tarbell pointed out three decades later in her autobiography, Roosevelt had "misread his Bunyan." In *The Pilgrim's Progress*, John Bunyan's muckraker symbolizes those who grub among the earthly world's "straws, and sticks, and dust" in quest of riches. The man with the muckrake refuses to surrender his muckrake—to relinquish this search for wealth—when offered in exchange the celestial crown of the path toward heaven.

As Tarbell explains it, she and her colleagues held the celestial crown of redemption, and the man with the muckrake represented corrupt corporate and political interests. Tarbell suggests in her memoir that Theodore Roosevelt believed that reform "should be left to him." Perhaps, she suggests, the President felt "a little resentment that a profession outside his own should be stealing his thunder."

Where did Roosevelt's speech leave *McClure's* and its branded journalists? Even as Steffens and Ida Tarbell had been examining lawlessness in America's businesses and cities, other staff writers had followed their own investigative trails. Their colleague Ray Stannard Baker had examined labor issues, race relations, lynching, the meatpacking industry, and railroad freight rates.

Other journalists had supplied *McClure's* with exposés on timber fraud, organized crime, and prostitution. The usual blend of fiction, poetry, history, popular science, and exploration had rounded out the magazine's pages. McClure persisted with this tested editorial formula in the years following Roosevelt's muckraker speech, but his publication never matched its past performance.

> "If the whole picture is painted black there remains no hue whereby to single out the rascals ... from their fellows."
> —THEODORE ROOSEVELT, APRIL 14, 1906
> DEFINING MUCKRAKER JOURNALISM

Nor did *McClure's* survive with its staff intact. By 1906—even as Roosevelt prepared to rock the foundations of reform journalism—the morale of *McClure's* writers rested on shaky ground. Over time a rift had opened between McClure and his staff. For starters, the editor's irrepressible energy and creativity created an environment full of tiresome distractions. Furthermore, his persistent schemes for expansion had grown so wild and grandiose that often they sounded as greedy and powerful as some of the industrial giants the journalists were battling with their typewriters and pens.

Talk was more hushed but no less critical on another point: McClure's attention to a contributing poet whom he seemed to favor for more reasons than her frequently published verse. How could the magazine speak with moral authority if its editor behaved indecently? Roosevelt's muckraking speech merely added to the confusion. Were the *McClure's* writers unwittingly muckrakers, with all of the negative associations the President had given to the word?

By midsummer more than half-a-dozen staff members had left *McClure's* to found their own magazine. Perhaps they thought a fresh start would erase the branding of "muckraker." They bought an existing periodical that had been recently renamed *the American Magazine*. The team announced plans to create "the most delightful monthly book ... [of] joyous reading that is anywhere published. It will reflect a happy, struggling, fighting world in which, as we believe, good people are coming out on top."

Their first issue, published in October 1906, and those that followed, proved remarkably similar to the old *McClure's*. Steffens wrote about West Coast politics; Tarbell explored topics of economics; Baker began a new series about race relations. The magazine examined the 12-hour workday of the steel industry, church corruption, and the life story of progressive politician Robert La Follette. As before, fiction, poetry, humor, history, and commentary rounded out the monthly issues.

McClure survived the mass exodus of his staff and continued to publish a varied editorial content that included muckraking. Among other topics, *McClure's* promoted the commissioner-based form of city government, the innovations of Italian educator Maria Montessori, and the end of "white slavery" (crime rackets that forced female immigrants to become prostitutes). McClure retired from publishing in 1911. His namesake magazine lived on until 1929—surpassing the half-million mark of circulation in 1918. *The American Magazine* survived as a voice for reform only until 1916. The former McClure's team had sold their financial interests—and unwittingly their editorial control—to outside investors. The magazine folded soon after.

In the years leading up to the demise of the *American* and *McClure's*—even as other magazines muckraked alongside of them—the literature of exposure gradually went out of fashion. Steffens and Baker both note in their memoirs that the public's interest in exposé was reaching the saturation point even before Roosevelt coined the term "muckraker" in April 1906. The President's speech undoubtedly hastened its decline in popularity, as did pressure from businesses. Through mass-market magazines like *McClure's,* businesses could advertise their products throughout the country. Over time, editors became dependent on the revenue from these product ads and grew cautious about criticizing companies that advertised in their publications. The journalists themselves were ready for other endeavors, too. Baker turned increasingly to commentary. Steffens, after two years at the *American,* became a freelance journalist. Tarbell wrote essays and biographies.

Muckraking journalists wield fountain-pen spears as they crusade against corruption in this 1906 cartoon. Participants include McClure's writers Ray Stannard Baker (foreground, behind shield), Lincoln Steffens (far right, on horseback), and Ida Tarbell (center, waving a magazine banner).

Ida Tarbell posed in 1912 at the American with some other McClure's veterans, including (standing, from left) Ray Stannard Baker and John Siddall (her Standard Oil research assistant), publisher John S. Phillips (seated, left), and managing editor Albert Boyden.

After Roosevelt left office in 1909, fellow Republican William Howard Taft sought to fill his role as a national reformer. His mixed results helped fuel the politically diverse election of 1912. That year Democrat Woodrow Wilson defeated Taft, Roosevelt (running on the Progressive Party ticket), and Socialist Party candidate Eugene Debs. Roosevelt's failed comeback was a blow to many loyal reformers and muckrakers. So was the emerging threat of international conflict. World War I increasingly diverted the nation and President Wilson away from progressive issues until they were largely forgotten. Not until the arrival in 1933 of the next President Roosevelt—Franklin D. Roosevelt—would reform come back into public and political favor.

Baker, writing to Steffens three years before this new Roosevelt took office, reminisced in his letter about the days "when we were both saving the world—so blithely!" The world hadn't been as easy to change as they'd imagined, he suggested. "We didn't know at the time quite how hard boiled it was."

Chapter 6

AN ENDURING TRADITION

Muckraking, like the push for reform, has become a tradition that ebbs and flows. In fact the two efforts usually resurface as a pair. Both may fall out of favor for a time, then erupt onto the scene just when most needed. The process starts with a breach of social justice. Smoldering concern follows. Then the determined writers exposé wrongs and inspire a swelling chorus of calls for change. These authors draw on important skills: courage, perseverance, confidence, persuasion. A lifetime of knowing the difference between right and wrong makes the perfect guide.

The muckraking style of newswriting came to be known as investigative journalism, or investigative reporting. Over time it has become a badge of honor to earn the title of muckraker, too. Even as newspapers and magazines have continued to introduce new investigative journalists through their pages, the tradition of muckraking has migrated into the evolving media of radio, television, and documentary film. Now, with a new century, the Internet extends this reach. An eclectic sampling of post-1912 muckraking yields an impressive variety of creators and content.

In 1914 Margaret Sanger, a nurse, turned to journalism in order to distribute information about birth control to ordinary citizens. She was charged with obscenity and threatened with prison for writing about this taboo subject. Sanger persevered, creating a periodical she named the *Woman Rebel,* even though she was jailed on eight occasions. She eventually created the nation's first family planning clinics.

John Steinbeck followed in the tradition of Upton Sinclair by writing *The Grapes of Wrath.* Not only did he research his book by shadowing the lives of his subjects—migrant workers during the 1930s—he presented his research in novel form, too. As with Sinclair, his searing portrait of worker exploitation caught the attention of a President named Roosevelt (Franklin D. Roosevelt). Steinbeck's book helped prompt early reform of migrant worker conditions. It earned him a Pulitzer Prize for literature in 1940 and became a major motion picture, as well.

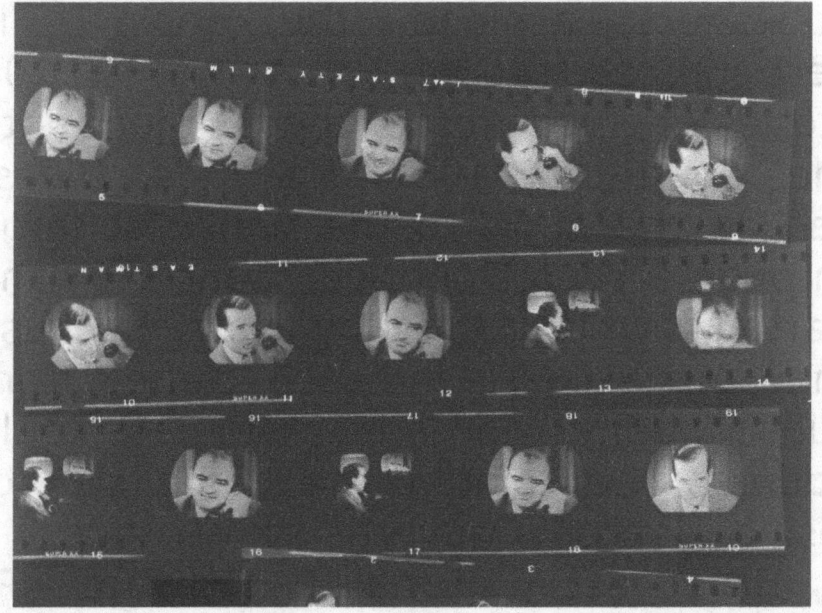

This photographer's contact sheet presents a sequence of still photos taken from Edward R. Murrow's news show, See It Now, the nation's first live coast-to-coast television program. On March 9, 1954, Murrow devoted an entire show to a report featuring excerpts of Senator Joseph McCarthy. At the end of the show, Murrow noted, "We must not confuse dissent with disloyalty." Americans were "defenders of freedom," he said, "but we cannot defend freedom abroad by deserting it at home."

Journalist George Seldes believed newspaper editors were censoring his hard-hitting stories, so in 1938 he founded his own weekly newspaper, *In Fact*. During the 1940s he wrote frequently about the hazards of smoking cigarettes at a time when other publishers avoided the topic. His persistence—through some 100 stories—helped force the subject into the open. In 1952 *Reader's Digest* carried the news to the public at large through a report entitled "Cancer by the Carton," written by Roy Norr. Because the magazine's income came from subscriptions, not advertising, it could address the topic without the risk of losing cigarette advertising revenue.

Broadcast journalist Edward R. Murrow covered World War II as a radio reporter and transitioned to television broadcasting as that medium took hold in the 1950s. He is most remembered for the series of reports he filed about Senator Joseph McCarthy for his *See It Now* feature on CBS-TV. The climactic episode of Murrow's series, which aired on March 9, 1954, prompted viewers to deluge the studio with 19 straight hours of phone calls and thousands of letters, almost all supportive of the program. It is often referred to as "television's finest hour." Murrow's gloves-off examination helped end the senator's obsessive, hearsay-based search for people who sympathized with the nation's Cold War enemy, the Soviet Union. Half a century later, this history inspired a major motion picture named after Murrow's signature closing line from his broadcasts, *Good Night, and Good Luck.*

"You may not be able to change the world but at least you can embarrass the guilty."
—JESSICA MITFORD
ADVICE TO ASPIRING
MUCKRAKERS

Four best-selling books carried on the tradition of muckraking during the 1960s even as television became an increasingly important source of breaking news. In *Silent Spring,* published in 1962, biologist and writer Rachel Carson uncovered the environmental damage being done by the increased use of pesticide chemicals. Published that same year, Michael Harrington's *The Other America: Poverty in the United States* called the nation's attention to the shocking incidence of poverty among some 50 million Americans, even those who held jobs. A year later Jessica Mitford exposed the manipulation of grieving customers by funeral home directors in *The American Way of Death.* Ralph Nader presented an equally damning picture of fraud within the automobile industry with his 1965 exposé *Unsafe at Any Speed: The Designed-in Dangers of the American Automobile.*

Carson's work led to the banning of the toxic chemical DDT and prompted the formation of the Environmental Protection Agency. Harrington's report contributed to the creation of such social welfare programs as Medicare, Medicaid, Head Start, and food stamps. Both books have been likened to *The Jungle* for their scope of revelations and their influence on legislation. Mitford's book promoted the first federal regulation of the funeral industry, and Nader's work led to passage of the

Traffic and Motor Vehicle Safety Act of 1966. This legislation authorized the federal government to regulate the auto industry for the first time and set minimum standards of safety for vehicles.

Muckraking continued in the late 1960s and early 1970s with two major exposés about the Vietnam War. In 1969 Seymour Hersh broke the news that U.S. soldiers had massacred civilians at a Vietnamese village named My Lai. Two years later *New York Times* reporter Neil Sheehan revealed the existence of a government study of the war's history, later known as the Pentagon Papers. Sheehan's work provoked a First Amendment showdown over freedom of the press that led all the way to the U.S. Supreme Court. At first a lower court order prevented publication of further stories, but this decision was overturned almost immediately by the Supreme Court in a landmark 6-3 ruling. The work of both journalists prompted greater scrutiny of the nation's involvement in the war and led to growing calls for its end.

Two reporters for the *Washington Post* reached the pinnacle of muckraking during the 1970s. Their two-year-long dogged search helped identify the political forces behind a break-in at the national headquarters for the Democratic Party, and its subsequent cover-up.

Rachel Carson's book Silent Spring drew the attention of federal lawmakers. In 1963 the scientist testified at Senate hearings about the risks of increased pesticide use. Humans and animals were being harmed, she said.

It took more than two reporters to force the resignation of President Richard M. Nixon in 1974. Other journalists, informants, lawmakers, judges, and even the Supreme Court, played a role. Still, Bob Woodward (left) and Carl Bernstein kept the Watergate story alive. Mounting evidence of lawlessness left the President with little choice• resign or face his likely removal from office by Congress.

What started as an insignificant police notice about an incident at the Watergate office complex on June 17, 1972, led Bob Woodward and Carl

Bernstein on the now-famous trail to the Oval Office of the White House. Their work contributed not only to the resignation of President Richard M. Nixon but to the criminal conviction of dozens of his associates as well. The pair filed 225 news stories, wrote two best-selling books, and inspired an Oscar-winning movie in the process.

In the final decades of the 20th century, muckrakers examined such diverse topics as the growing spread of AIDS among the gay community, stories about the Roman Catholic Church's cover-up of child molesting by priests, and new evidence in unsolved crimes from the civil rights era. The relevance and need for muckraking remained, even as the country began a new century. Muckrakers speak today from books, films, newspapers, radio, television, even the Internet.

Pay attention, urges Eric Schlosser in *Fast Food Nation—The Dark Side of the All-American Meal:* Anew jungle exists in the world of American slaughterhouses, where illegal immigrants labor without adequate health care, benefits, or protection.

Buyer beware, advise investigative journalists: You may be encouraged to purchase medication, treatment plans, or equipment that manufacturers know is unsafe.

Fix this injustice, demands William Glaberson in the *New York Times:* The town and village courts of New York State are staffed by amateur judges unschooled in the practice of law.

The uncensored circulation of photographs on the Internet from Abu Ghraib prison in Iraq helped exposé U.S.–led torturing of prisoners during the Iraq War. Traditional news sources documented the heat, overcrowding, and poor conditions in the prison (about, July 2003) but failed to uncover the extent of the abuse.

Things are not what they seem, warns Seymour Hersh in *Chain of Command—The Road from g/u to Abu Ghraib:* Arrogance, poor planning, and disregarded advice helped compromise success in the Iraq War.

Don't be deceived, reports Dana Priest in the *Washington Post:* The U.S. government has created secret detention centers overseas so that suspected terrorists may be interrogated and tortured beyond the reach of international law.

All is not well, Priest and Anne Hull reveal later in the *Post:* Wounded Iraq War soldiers are seriously neglected during outpatient treatment at the Walter Reed Army Medical Center in Washington, D.C.

The Internet extends the reach of warning and dissent. It provides an alternative outlet when traditional media find themselves constrained by corporate owners or by the threat of lost advertising revenues. It enables everyday citizens—not just professional journalists—to speak their minds. Web sites, e-mails, blogs, and media-sharing forums like YouTube and MySpace offer new ways to connect with an audience that spans the globe and is more diverse than ever before.

In 1920 Ray Stannard Baker reminisced about old times in a letter to a former colleague: "I suppose they will return again, such times of awakening," he wrote. "Others will return, I am confident, to the task which seemed once almost a mission and a call."

Ida Tarbell, Upton Sinclair (top), and Lincoln Steffens in their later years.

Afterword

"It is the job of a newspaperman to spur the lazy, watch the weak, exposé the corrupt," observed Drew Pearson. This journalist, following in the footsteps of the first muckrakers, uncovered everything from political corruption in Louisiana during the 1930s to the news that General George S. Patton had slapped a shell-shocked soldier during World War II. His words sum up the convictions of the founding voices of investigative journalism.

Those writers—from Lincoln Steffens to Ida Tarbell to Upton Sinclair and so many others—led a revolution with their pens at the turn of the 20th century. Perhaps growing up in the shadow of Abraham Lincoln's legacy inspired them to champion the cause of social justice with their inky voices. Surely some childlike curiosity fueled their commitment to always learn and study, forever piece together the mystery of how the world works. Their writing helped tie the nation together with words and beliefs, just as the railroads had united it geographically. As outsiders they could more easily speak up about matters of local concern and connect these issues to national patterns. All of these qualities added to their genius and to their role as a positive force for change.

This winning chemistry gave results. As one historian notes: "The group changed things, and few writers can claim that." Not only did these first muckrakers influence government reform, they helped shift the country from one with state-centered power to one based on national control. They gave voice to new political movements, such as socialism and progressive politics. Their work helped establish journalism as a profession: schools of journalism opened in their wake. Inadvertently the muckrakers spurred the creation of a new industry, too—public relations. They may even have prompted the nation's most wealthy citizens to give away more of their fortunes in hopes of improving their personal images and family names.

Upton Sinclair, one of the youngest muckrakers, lived to be one of the oldest. Only his death in 1968 at age 90 put an end to his writing. By then he had more than 90 novels, books of nonfiction, and plays to his credit. His devotion to socialism ebbed over time, and in 1934 he resigned from the Socialist Party to run for governor of California as a Democrat. (He lost.) When not writing, Sinclair experimented with fad diets, established a communal living center, and helped found the American Civil Liberties Union. In 1942 one of his "Lanny Budd" historical spy novels earned a Pulitzer Prize for literature. *The Jungle* remains in print and is often studied in college courses about history and literature; it has been translated into more than 40 languages.

Inspectors helped assure the quality of military rations for World War I. Cans of spoiled meat had caused illness and even death during the Spanish-American War of 1898.

The remorseful tone that John D. Rockefeller, Jr., adopted at federal hearings in 1915 (above) removed some of the tarnish from the family name.

Any tensions that accompanied the staff split at *McClure's* in 1906 faded as time passed. Reporters kept in touch as friends, and many of them renewed contacts with their former boss, S.S. McClure. Tarbell includes in her autobiography the fond remembrance of a gathering some of them shared when he turned 78. She writes: "We all sat down together as once we had sat down in the old ... lunching places." The friends gathered, "enthralled as in the old years while Mr. McClure enlarged on his latest enthusiasm, marveling as always at the eternal youthfulness in the man, the failure of life to quench him." During his remaining years, McClure pursued his interest in publishing and world peace. He died in 1949 at the age of 92.

Lincoln Steffens *did* make his name with *The Shame of the Cities*, as he had predicted. He went on to investigate politics on the West Coast, revolutions in Europe, and unrest at home. He supported Democratic Party candidate Woodrow Wilson in 1913 (instead of Theodore Roosevelt or other candidates) but examined socialism and communism at times in his life, too. Steffens devoted five years to the writing of his autobiography, an 800-plus-page classic of the genre. He lived to be 70 years old, dying in 1936.

Rockefeller biographer Ron Chernow observes that *The History of the Standard Oil Company* by Ida Tarbell "remains one of the great case studies of what a single journalist, armed with the facts, can do against seemingly invincible powers." When asked in later years what she would change if she could revise the book, her emphatic reply was: "Not one word, young man, not one word." Tarbell, who never married, worked when few women held professional posts. She wrote for the rest of her life, penning essays of social commentary, biographies, and her own engaging autobiography. Gardening brought her a lifetime of pleasure. Her fame far outlasted her death in 1944 at age 86. Nearly 60 years later the U.S. Postal Service honored her on a postage stamp as one of four notable women journalists. (Early muckraker Nellie Bly was another, along with Marguerite Higgins and Ethel L. Payne.)

Ray Stannard Baker wrote essays and fiction before turning to government service during President Woodrow Wilson's administration. Among other duties he served as a sort of press secretary for the President during treaty negotiations after World War I. Then Baker returned to his pen as the biographer of his former boss. Over time he authored an eight-volume study called *Woodrow Wilson: Life and Letters.* In 1940 he earned a Pulitzer Prize for the last two books in the series. He died in 1946 at age 76.

When he assumed the Presidency in 1901, Theodore Roosevelt pledged not to serve more than one additional term in office (approximately the equivalent of the eight-year precedent set by George Washington). With some reluctance he honored that pledge by leaving office with the election of 1908. Disappointment in the leadership of his hand-picked successor, William Howard Taft, prompted his comeback bid in 1912 as a Progressive Party candidate. He lost the race to Woodrow Wilson. Roosevelt filled his retirement years with safaris in Africa, an expedition to the jungles of Brazil, and writing. He had more than 30 books to his credit by the end of his life in 1919 at age 60.

Roosevelt may have coined the term "muckraker," but investigative journalists of that era had the last word. Historians agree that the "Treason of the Senate" series by David Graham Phillips contributed to the ratification in 1913 of the 17th Amendment. This legislation changed the U.S. Constitution so that senators would be elected directly by voters, as they are today, not by state legislatures. Furthermore, by the time the amendment took effect, 17 of the 21 senators whom Phillips had exposéd as corrupt were gone from office. Unfortunately, Phillips, gunned down by an assassin in 1911, did not live to see the far-reaching effects his writing had.

It took a series of rulings at the state and U.S. Supreme Court levels to test and secure Theodore Roosevelt's expansion of federal authority. His leadership—bolstered by the work of investigative journalists—set the stage for the modern era of government. Echoes of those earliest federal laws continue to be heard. The Sherman Antitrust Act—so extensively tested during Roosevelt's administration—remains a potent tool for curbing the growth of monopolies. The Pure Food and Drug Act of 1906 still serves as the basis of the nation's food safety net. When President Lyndon B. Johnson signed into law the

Wholesome Meat Act of 1967, an expansion of that federal authority, he included Upton Sinclair, age 89, at the signing ceremony.

"I realized early that what a man or a woman does is built on what those who gone before have done ... its real value depends on making the matter in hand a little clearer, a little sounder for those who come after."
—IDA TARBELL, 1939
FROM HER AUTOBIOGRAPHY, *ALL IN THE DAY'S WORK*

Sixty-one years and ten Presidents after influencing the passage of the Pure Food and Drug Act, Upton Sinclair returned to the White

House for the signing of a companion bill by President Lyndon B. Johnson (above, left, shaking hands with Sinclair). Among others attending was auto-safety advocate Ralph Nader; the pair of muckrakers talked after the ceremony.

Inevitably, new inequities develop in a changing world, and new muckrakers must emerge to take up the call of social justice. As was the case 100 years ago, journalists continue to serve as that unofficial fourth branch of government—balancing the nation's legislative, judicial, and executive actions. Their voices, at their best, are right but not righteous, empowering without being overpowering. They serve as a positive force for hope and change. Perhaps Charles Edward Russell, a muckraking contemporary of the *McClure's* writers, sums up the goals shared then and in the years since: "There is no such thing in this world as a wasted protest against any existing evil."

Time Line of Muckraking and Pantheon of Muckrakers

The following time line presents a sampling of muckraking from the history of journalism and is by no means an exhaustive record of all such work. Key publishing and political events are included. Profiles of notable muckrakers accompany the time line. Taken together these writers form a pantheon—a sort of honor roll-worthy of admiration, respect, and appreciation.

1858

An article called "The Swill Milk Trade of New York and Brooklyn" runs in the May 8 issue of *Frank Leslie's Illustrated Newspaper,* exposing the production of poor-quality milk among city-raised cows that are fed swill (a by-product of fermentation) instead of adequate grain.

1859

The first oil well is drilled near Titusville, Penn.

The publication of Charles Darwin's *Origin of Species* prompts many intellectuals to emphasize the philosophical teachings of the Bible and defer to Darwin for scientific explanations about the origins of life.

1872

In "The King of Frauds," the *New York Sun* details the unscrupulous dealings of financiers through Credit Mobilier during the construction of the transcontinental railroad. Published on September 4, the article implicates more than a dozen U.S. congressmen and prompts a federal investigation of the scandal during 1873.

Nellie Bly
Born: May 5, 1864, in Cochran's Mills, Penn., with the name Elizabeth Jane Cochran
Death: January 27, 1922, in New York, N.Y., age 57
Muckraking and other writing: Using Bly, this enterprising journalist gained fame by posing as an inmate in order to report on the treatment of women in a mental hospital. She wrote undercover stories about prison life, child labor, and the selling of babies, too. In 1889, on behalf of the *New York World,* she raced to beat the fictional record set in the Jules Verne novel *Around the World in 80 Days.* She completed her journey in just over 72 days. Years later she became the first woman to file battle

reports from World War I's eastern front.

Quotable remarks: *"Energy rightly applied and directed will accomplish anything."*

1887

Nellie Bly spends "Ten Days in a Mad-House" disguised as a patient in order to observe mistreatment of the mentally ill as background for her series in the *New York World,* which starts on October 16.

Jacob Riis
Born: May 3, 1849, in Ribe, Denmark
Death: May 26, 1914, in Barre, Mass., age 65

Muckraking and other writing: Jacob Riis may be best known for *How the Other Half Lives* (1890), an illustrated exposé of ghetto life in lower Manhattan during the 19th century. His other muckraking books include *The Children of the Poor* (1892), *Out of Mulberry Street* (1898), and *The Battle with the Slum* (1902). He titled his autobiography, published in 1901. *The Making of an American.*

Quotable remarks: *"The sea of a mighty population ... heaves uneasily in the tenements. The gap between the classes ... is widening day by day. I know of but one bridge that will carry us over safe, a bridge founded upon justice and built of human hearts."*

1888

On September 2 the *San Francisco Examiner* publishes "Overboard: An 'Examiner' Man Tests the Life-Saving Gear of the Ferry."

1890

Scribner's publishes *How the Other Half Lives*, a study on ghetto life in New York City by Jacob Riis.

1892

Ida B. Wells (later Ida B. Wells-Barnett) reports on May 21 in the Memphis newspaper Free *Speech* about the horror and injustice of racially motivated lynching. After her newspaper offices are destroyed in retaliation, she leaves the South and takes her story to the *New York Age.*

1893

S.S. McClure founds *McClure's Magazine* in New York, NY., with J.S. Phillips and associates.

1894

Henry Demarest Lloyd writes a documentary about J.D. Rockefeller and the development of Standard Oil.

1895

Theodore Roosevelt is appointed a commissioner of the New York City Police Board. Lincoln Steffens covers Roosevelt's reform efforts for the *Commercial Advertiser.* Roosevelt resigns in April 1897 to become President William McKinley's Assistant Secretary of the Navy.

Ida B. Well-Barnett
Born: July 16, 1862, in Holly Springs, Miss.
Death: March 25, 1931, in Chicago, Ill., age 68
Muckraking and other writing: Ida B. Wells wrote her first stories about the Americans in 1892 for her Memphis newspaper *Free Speech.* Mob violence stopped publication and forced

her to leave Tennessee and move to New York. Later on, she became the first African-American journalist for the *Chicago Inter-Ocean* and wrote for the black-owned *Chicago Conservator*. Known as Wells-Barnett after her marriage, she helped found the NAACP and sought voting rights for women, too.

Quotable remarks: "I'd rather go down in history as one lone Negro who dared to tell the government that it had done a dastardly thing than to save my skin by taking back what I have said."

S.S. McClure
Born: Feb.17, 1857, in County Antrim, Ireland

Death: March 21, 1949, in New York, N.Y., age 92

Muckraking and other writing: Samuel Sidney McClure founded a literary syndicate in 1884 that matched writers on both sides of the Atlantic with opportunities for simultaneous publication in newspapers and magazines across the U.S. In 1893 he established the monthly *McClure's Magazine*. Novelist Willa Cather helped ghostwriter his autobiography. It ran in serial from in *McClure's* before being published as a book in 1914.

Quotable remarks: *"people often ask me how I got ideas for the magazine. An editor, of course, gets ideas from his interest in what is going on in the world; being interested is a large part of an editor's vocational equipment."*

1898

The Spanish-American War is fought to determine the independence of Cuba. Theodore Roosevelt participates as a colonel, leading his regiment of Rough Riders. Media coverage related to the war becomes increasingly sensational and provocative, prompting Joseph Pulitzer to retreat from his commitment to print shocking and exaggerated news.

1899

Packingtown, an early exposé about the meatpacking industry in Chicago by Algie Simmons, is published by Charles H. Kerr & Co.

The *Chicago Daily Tribune* gathers statistics on injuries caused by fireworks in an article warning of their use during Independence Day celebrations.

1902

William McKinley is assassinated on September 14; Theodore Roosevelt becomes the nation's 36th President.

1902

"Tweed Days in St. Louis" runs in the October issue *of McClure's Magazine* as the first installment of what becomes known as *The Shame of the Cities* by

Lincoln Steffens. Book publication follows in 1904.

The first installment of Ida Tarbell's *The History of the Standard Oil Company* appears in the November issue of *McClure's*. The collected articles are published as a two-volume book set in 1904.

1903

The January issue of *McClure's* includes an editorial calling attention to its three articles about "American Contempt of the Law." They are authored by Ray Stannard Baker, Lincoln Steffens, and Ida Tarbell.

1904

Wall Street insider Thomas Lawson writes a tell-all exposé called "Frenzied Finance" for the August issue of *Everybody's Magazine*.

Edward Bok publishes a series of editorials warning about "The 'Patent-Medicine' Curse" in the *Ladies' Home Journal*.

Republican Party candidate Theodore Roosevelt becomes the first President by succession to gain outright election to the Presidency with his defeat of Alton Brooks Parker, a Democrat.

Lincoln Steffens
Born: April 6, 1866, in San Francisco, Calif.
Death: Aug.9, 1936, in Carmel, Calif., age 70
Muckraking and other writing: Lincoln Steffens began his writing career in 1892 as a financial reporter for the New York Evening Post. He partnered on the revival of the city's Commercial Advertiser, too. Steffens joined the staff of McClure's in 1902. His series on civic corruption, The Shame of the Cities, ran from October 1902 to November 1903 before it book publication in 1904. The Struggle for Self-Government, his look at the

"Shame of the States," appeared as a collection two years later. His classic *Autobiography* was published in 1931.

Quotable remarks: *"You may beat the public to the news, not to the truth."*

Ida M. Tarbell

Born: Nov.5, 1857, in Erie County, Penn.

Death: Jan.6, 1944, in Bridgeport, Conn., age 86

Muckraking and other writing: Ida Minerva Tarbell joined the staff of *McClure's* in 1894. In addition to her series about Standard Oil, Tarbell authored biographies for the magazine about Napoleon Bonaparte and Abraham Lincoln. She published her final muckraking in 1911—a collection of articles on the disadvantages of import tariffs, or taxes. She titled her 1939 autobiography *All in the Day's Work.*

Quotable remarks: *"There was born in me a hatred of privilege.... It was well, at fifteen, to have one definite plank based on things seen and heard, ready for a future platform of social and economic justice if I should ever awake to my need of one."*

1905

The British medical journal *The Lancet* publishes "The Dark and Insanitary-Premises Used for the Slaughtering of Cattle and Hogs," by Adolphe Smith on January 14.

The *Appeal to Reason* begins serial publication of Upton Sinclair's novel *The Jungle.* The final installment appears on November 4.

Ray Stannard Baker examines corrupt "Railroad Rebates" in the December issue of *McClure's.* Four additional articles follow, including one called "Railroads on Trial" in the March 1906 issue.

Thomas Lawson examines fraud in the life insurance industry through a series for *Everybody's Magazine.*

Publication begins in *Collier's* magazine of a serial by Samuel Hopkins Adams about "The Great American Fraud" of patent medicines.

Charles Edward Russell examines the meatpacking industry in his book *The Greatest Trust in the World* published by the Ridgeway-Thayer Co.

1906

Upton Sinclair's *The Jungle* is published as a book by Doubleday, Page and Co., during February.

Cosmopolitan Magazine begins publication of the "Treason of the Senate" series by David Graham Phillips in March.

President Theodore Roosevelt coins the term "muckraker" during a speech in Washington, D.C., on April 14, having first tested his remarks on March 17 at a private dinner for journalists who were members of the Gridiron Club.

Ray Stannard Baker

Born: April 17, 1870, in lansing, Mich.

Death: July 12, 1946, in Amherst, Mass., age 76

Muckraking and other writing: Ray Stannard Baker joined the staff of *McClure's Magazine* in 1898. He pieces for it and the *American Magazine* about race relations, management and labor issues, child labor, and railroad companies. He used the pen named David Grayson to write human interest essays about simple living, such as *Adventures in Contentment* (1907). Baker kept a diary for nearly 50 years; it grew to a length of some two million words by the end of his life.

Quotable remarks: "We were ourselves personally astonished, personally ashamed, personally indignant at what we found, and we wrote earnestly, even hotly. [Years later] one other point impresses me sadly.... we are still far from the democracy of our vision."

McClure's Magazine publishes an examination of "The Story of Life Insurance" in a series by Burton J. Hendrick beginning in May.

Former staff members from *McClure's* reorganize under the banner of the *American Magazine* during July. Their first issue is published in October.

Edwin Markham writes a series about child labor entitled "The Hoe-Man in the Making" beginning with the September issue of *Cosmopolitan Magazine.*

George Kibbe Turner writes about the commissioner form of government in "Galveston: A Business Corporation" for the October issue of *McClure's.*

1907

George Kibbe Turner's article on vice in the city of Chicago, published in the April issue of *McClure's,* helps prompt Illinois to establish the first state minimum wage laws.

The American *Magazine* publishes Ray Stannard Baker's article in May, entitled "Clash of Races in a Southern City," as part of a series on race relations that is later published by Doubleday, Page and Co., as *Following the Color Line* (1908).

Brand Whitlockwrites a novel condemning capital punishment called *The Turn of the Balance.*

1908

The June issue of *Everybody's Magazine* carries Charles Edward Russell's exposé about how the state of Georgia leases its prisoners to contractors as free labor in exchange for providing their room and board.

Charles Edward Russell explores the hypocritical connection between Trinity Church and the huge revenues it nets as owner of extensive slum tenements in NewYork City. The piece runs in the July issue *of Everybody's;* similar pieces appear in other muckraking magazines around the same time.

Edward Bok examines the taboo subject of venereal disease in a photo-illustrated series for the *Ladies' Home Journal.* Subscriptions fall by 70,000 readers in protest, but the series leads ultimately to greater openness about discussing sex.

1909

Documentary photographs by Lewis Hine of children working in factories contribute to the demand for child labor protection laws.

In November *McClure's* exposes the white slave trade of immigrants caught up in prostitution in "The Daughters of the Poor" by George Kibbe Turner.

1911

John A. Fitch writes about the 12-hour workday of the steel industry in "Old Age at Forty" for the March issue of the *American Magazine.*

S.S. McClure retires as editor of *McClure's Magazine.* The magazine survives until 1929.

1912

Former chief executive Theodore Roosevelt stages a political comeback as the Progressive Party candidate for President. He garners more votes than Republican President William Howard Taft, but is defeated by Democrat Woodrow Wilson.

1913

The ratification of the 17th Amendment places the election of U.S. senators into the hands of voters, not state legislators as had previously been stipulated in the U.S. Constitution.

1914

Edwin Markham writes an exposé about child labor, *Children in Bondage.*

Margaret Sanger campaigns for greater access to information about birth control by founding the *Woman Rebel.* Her periodical is labeled obscene, and

Sanger is forced to flee the country or face imprisonment.

Upton Sinclair
Born: Sept.20, 1878, in Baltimore, Md.
Death: Nov.25, 1968, in Bound Brook, N.J., age 90
Muckraking and other writing: Upton Beall Sinclair examined meatpackers such as Ogden Armour in his Novel *The Jungle,* the Rockefeller family with his novel and stage play named *Oil!* (first published in 1927), and Henry Ford through his 1937 novel *The Flivver King*. "I have reformed three American families in my writing: the Armours, the Rockefellers, and the Ford," observed Sinclair. The muckraker made several unsuccessful attempts to run for office,

as governor of California, U.S. senator, and U.S. congressman.

Quotable remarks: *"I don't know whether anyone will care to examine my heart [when I die], but if they do they will find two words there—'Social Justice.'"*

1916

Outside investors assume control of the *American Magazine;* it folds soon after.

1919

Sports fan and journalist Hugh Fullerton questions: "Is Big League Baseball Being Run for Gamblers, With Ballplayers in the Deal?" His story appears December 15 in the *New York World* and prompts an investigation; revelations follow that White Sox players had deliberately lost the 1919 World Series as part of a betting scheme.

1931

Drew Pearson publishes *Washington Merry-Go-Round* and goes on to prepare a regular column with that name for the *Washington Post;* in it he exposes political corruption during a reporting career that spans four decades.

1938

George Seldes founds *In Fact,* a weekly newspaper, to avoid censorship in the mainstream media. He uses this forum to help exposé the hazards of cigarette smoking.

1939

The Grapes of Wrath calls attention to the hardships of migrant labor when John Steinbeck's novel is published by Viking Press.

1942

Publication in November of a report about Nazi death camps by the *Jewish Frontier* fails to gain the attention of the mainstream press. Not until the ending of World War II in 1945 would the full story of Nazi concentration camps be reported.

1952

Reader's Digest publishes "Cancer by the Carton" in its December issue, an article by Roy Norr about the health hazards of smoking cigarettes.

1953

On October 20 Edward R. Murrow initiates his hard-hitting look at Senator Joseph McCarthy for *See It Now* on CBS-TV. A noted episode runs on March 9, 1954. His series leads to the senator's censure and helps to end his sensational hunt for Communist sympathizers.

1959

"The Safe Car You Can't Buy" appears in *The Nation* on April 11 as an early exposé by Ralph Nader about automobile design flaws.

1960

In April *Sepia* magazine begins publishing a series of articles by John Howard Griffin, a white reporter who spends five weeks disguised as a black man to examine race relations in the South.

Edward R. Murrow
Born: April 25, 1908, near Greensboro, N.C., with the name Egbert Roscoe Murrow
Death: April 27, 1965, near Pawling, N.Y., age 57
Muckraking and other writing: During World War II, Edward R. Murrow made his name as a radio broadcaster from besieged London. He entered the new medium of television news after the war. His *See It Now*

program set the standard for television newsmagazines and aired weekly from 1951 to 1958. His 1960 "Harvest of Shame" documentary about exploited migrant farm workers inspired legislation and other films.

Quotable remarks: *"We will not walk in fear, one of another.... Remember that we are not descended from fearful men, not from men who feared to write, to speak, to associate and to defend causes which were for the moment unpopular."*

Rachel Carson
Born: May 27, 1907, in Springdale, Penn.
Death: April 14, 1964, in Silver Spring, Md., age 56

Muckraking and other writing: Rachel Carson's landmark book about the environmental hazards of pesticide use, *Silent Spring,* was published in 1962. Prior to book publication it appeared as a serial in the *New Yorker* magazine. Carson had gained fame even earlier with a series of three books about the seas and shoreline. The second volume of this trilogy earned her a National Book Award in 1951. Carson defended her *Silent Spring* research at Congressional hearings even as she battled to overcome breast cancer, the disease that ultimately claimed her life.

Quotable remarks: *"No witchcraft, no enemy action had silenced the rebirth of new life in this stricken world. The people had done it themselves."*

1962

Michael Harrington's study of poverty in *The Other America: Poverty in the United States* is published by Macmillan.

Silent Spring by Rachel Carson prompts government action on environmental protection following its publication by Houghton Mifflin.

1963

Simon and Schuster publishes *The American Way of Death* by Jessica Mitford, an exposé of fraudulent practices in the funeral industry.

1969

Ralph Nader's *Unsafe at Any Speed: The Designed-in Dangers of the American Automobile* is published in November by Grossman Publishers. His revelations prompt the federal government to establish its first automobile safety standards by the next year.

1969

Seymour Hersh breaks the story of the My Lai massacre from the Vietnam War through a November story distributed by the Dispatch News Service.

1971

Reporting for the *New York Times,* Neil Sheehan discloses on June 13 the existence of a Vietnam War study by the Pentagon. A court battle ensues before the Supreme Court asserts the newspaper's First Amendment right to publish the Pentagon Papers.

1972

Writing for the *Washington Post* on February 39, Jack Anderson reveals the connection between a corporate campaign contribution to the Republican Party and the subsequent dismissal of an antitrust suit against that company by the Republican administration of President Richard M. Nixon.

On June 19 Carl Bernstein and Bob Woodward publish their first cowritten article in the *Washington Post* of a two-year series of stories about a June burglary of offices at the Watergate building. Their reports contribute to the resignation of President Richard M. Nixon on August 9, 1974.

"Syphilis Patients Died Untreated" reports Jean Heller in an Associated Press story from July 25. The story reveals that African-American men unwittingly participated in a 40-year experiment to study the characteristics of syphilis when it is treated and when it is left untreated.

1974

Seymour Hersh uncovers the practice of illegal domestic spying by the CIA in a *New York Times* story on December 22.

1975

Ms magazine publishes a report in its April issue by B.J. Phillips about the mysterious death of Karen Silkwood following her investigation into radiation exposure as a nuclear power plant employee.

1983

Larry Kramer widens public awareness of the spread of AIDS through a story called "1, 112 and

Counting" for the March 14-37 issue of the *New York Native.*

1985

The *National Catholic Reporter* begins reporting about child abuse by priests and a church cover-up of the matter, in its July 7 issue.

1986

Syndicated columnist Jack Anderson discloses that the administration of President Ronald Reagan has sold weapons to Iran in order to influence the release of political hostages in the Middle East.

Bob Woodward (right) and Carl Bernstein

Woodward born: March 26, 1943, in Geneva, Ill.

Bernstein born: Feb. 14, 1944, in Washington, D.C.

Muckraking and other writing: The investigative reports about Watergate by Bob Woodward and Carl Bernstein helped earn a Pulitzer Prize for the *Washington Post* in 1973. The pair collaborated in two related books: *All the President's Men* (1974), a chronicle of their investigations, and *The Final Days* (1976), an account of the ending of the Nixon Presidency. They have written since for newspapers, magazines, and book publishers on topics ranging from the Supreme Court and other Presidents (Woodward) to Pope John Paul II (Bernstein).

Quotable remarks: *"There are always unanswered questions.... There never is a final draft of history."—Bob Woodward*

"Reporters may believe they control the story, but the story always controls the reporters."—Carl Bernstein

1987

Bob Woodward exposés questionable policies and practices at the Central Intelligence Agency in *Veil: The Secret Wars of the CIA 19.81–1987.*

1989

Jerry Mitchell reports on October 1 in the Jackson, Miss., *Clarion-Ledger* that the 1964 trial of the man accused of assassinating civil rights leader Medgar Evers was rigged with jury tampering. His story leads to the reopening of the case and a murder conviction. Other civil rights cases from the era are reexamined and retried in following years.

1993

Eileen Welsome exposés "The Plutonium Experiment," a federal study involving plutonium injections conducted without patient knowledge. It runs on November 15 in the *Albuquerque Tribune.*

2001

Eric Schlosser examines the health hazards of convenience foods in *Fast Food Nation: The Dark Side of the All-American Meal,* published by Houghton Mifflin.

2004

Seymour Hersh collects a series written for the *New Yorker* magazine about the government's Iraq War policy into a book called *Chain of Command: The Road from 9/11 to Abu Ghraib.*

2005

Dana Priest, reporting in November for the *Washington Post,* uncovers the existence of secret overseas detention centers maintained by the CIA for its fight against terrorism.

2006

William Glaberson writes a three-part series for the *New York Times* about the "Broken Bench" of New York State's system of 1,250 town and village courts.

Bob Woodward publishes State *of Denial*, the third book in his investigative look at the planning and execution of the Iraq War under the leadership of President George W. Bush. He documents systematic negligence and misjudgment.

Seymour Hersh
Born: April 8, 1937, in Chicago, Ill.
Muckraking and other writing: Seymour Hersh began his Journalistic career as a police reporter in Chicago in 1959. Ten years later he gained reporting fame with his investigative reports about the massacre of unarmed civilians at the village of My

Lai in Vietnam by U.S. troops. His articles earned him a Pulitzer Prize. Hersh went on to investigate Watergate and other and other stories for the *New York Times* before becoming a freelance writer. His subsequent books and articles for such magazines as the *Atlantic Monthly* and the *New Yorker* have broken news about everything from controversial Central Intelligence Agency operations to veterans' illnesses following the Gulf War to the torture by Americans of Iraqis at Abu Ghraib prison.

Quotable remarks: "You have to not be afraid to tell the truth."

2007

In a follow-up report for the *New York Times,* William Glaberson reveals widespread fraud and mismanagement of the millions of dollars exchanging hands each year in New York State's small-town courts.

Washington Post reporters Dana Priest and Anne Hull exposé widespread problems with outpatient care at the

Walter Reed Army Medical Center for soldiers wounded in the Iraq War.

Resource Guide

Recommended Books by Muckrakers

Baker, Ray Stannard. *American Chronicle: The Autobiography of Ray Stannard Baker.* New York: Charles Scribner's Sons, 1945.

Bernstein, Carl, and Bob Woodward. *All the President's Men.* New York: Simon & Schuster, 1974.

Sinclair, Upton. *The Autobiography of Upton Sinclair.* New York: Harcourt, Brace & World, Inc., 1962.

_____. *The Jungle: The Uncensored Original Edition.* Tucson, Arizona: See Sharp Press, 2003.

_____, edited by Clare Virginia Eby. *The Jungle: A Norton Critical Edition.* New York: W.W. Norton & Company, Inc., 2003.

Steffens, Lincoln. *The Autobiography of Lincoln Steffens.* New York: Harcourt, Brace and Company, Inc., 1931.

Tarbell, Ida M. *All in the Day's Work: An Autobiography.* New York: The Macmillan Company, 1939.

Annotated Collections of Muckraking

Jensen, Carl (editor). *Stories That Changed America: Muckrakers of the 20th Century.* New York: Seven Stories Press, 2000.

Weinberg, Arthur, and Lila Weinberg (editors). *The Muckrakers.* Urbana: University of Illinois Press, 1961, 2001.

Muckraking at the Movies

All the President's Men, Alan Pakula (director), starring Dustin Hoffman (Carl Bernstein) and Robert Redford (Bob Woodward), 1976.

Good Night, and Good Luck, George Clooney (director), starring David Strathairn (Edward R. Murrow), 2005.

Grapes of Wrath, John Ford (director), starring Henry Fonda (Tom Joad), 1940.

Places to Visit in Person and Online

DRAKE WELL MUSEUM

202 Museum Lane, Titusville, PA 16354 http://www.drakewell.org/

NEWSEUM

Interactive museum of news Pennsylvania Avenue (at 6th Street) Washington, D.C. http://www.newseum.org/

PROJECT CENSORED

Reports of "the news that didn't make the news" http://www.projectcensored.org/

PROJECT FOR EXCELLENCE IN JOURNALISM

http://www.journalism.org/

PULITZER PRIZE

http://www.pulitzer.org/

SOCIETY OF PROFESSIONAL JOURNALISTS http://www.spj.org/

IDA TARBELL

http://tarbell.alleg.edu/

THE WATERGATE STORY

http://www.washiiigtonpost.com/wp-srv/onpolitics/watergate/splash.html

Bibliography

Arthur, Anthony. *Radical Innocent: Upton Sinclair.* New York: Random House, 2006.

Baker, Ray Stannard. *American Chronicle: The Autobiography of Ray Stannard Baker.* New York: Charles Scribner's Sons, 1945.

Bernstein, Carl, and Bob Woodward. *All the President's Men.* New York: Simon & Schuster, 1974.

Brady, Kathleen. *Ida Tarbell: Portrait of a Muckraker.* Pittsburgh, Penn.: University of Pittsburgh Press, 1989.

Bunyan, John. *The Pilgrim's Progress.* New York: The Macmillan Company, 1948.

Chalmers, David Mark. *The Muckrake Years.* New York: D. Van Nostrand Company, 1974.

_____. *The Social and Political Ideas of the Muckrakers.* New York: The Citadel Press, 1964.

Chernow, Bon. *Titan: The Life of John D. Rockefeller, Sr.* New York: Random House, 1998.

Crunden, Robert M. *Ministers of Reform: The Progressives' Achievement in American Civilization, 1880–1920.* New York: Basic Books, Inc., 1982.

Eby, Clare Virginia (editor). *The Jungle: A Norton Critical Edition.* New York: W.W. Norton & Company, Inc., 2003.

Folkerts, Jean, and Dwight L. Teeter, Jr. *Voices of a Nation: A History of Mass Media in the United States.* Boston: Allyn & Bacon, 2002 (fourth edition).

Jensen, Carl (editor). *Stories That Changed America: Muckrakers of the 20th Century.* New York: Seven Stories Press, 2000.

Kochersberger, Robert C, Jr., (editor). Afore *Than a Muckraker: Ida Tarbell's Lifetime in Journalism.* Knoxville: The University of Tennessee Press, 1994.

Kroeger, Brooke. *Nellie Bly: Daredevil, Reporter, Feminist.* New York: Times Books, Random House, 1994.

Mattson, Kevin. *Upton Sinclair and the Other American Century.* Hoboken, N.J.: John Wiley & Sons, Inc., 2006.

McClure, S.S. *My Autobiography.* New York: Frederick Ungar Publishing Co., 1963.

McClure's Magazine, Volumes 20-23, 1902-1904.

McGerr, Michael. *A Fierce Discontent: The Rise and Fall of the Progressive Movement in America, 1870-1920.* New York: Oxford University Press, 2003.

Morris, Edmund. *The Rise of Theodore Roosevelt.* New York: The Modern Library, 1981.

_____. *Theodore Rex.* New York: Random House, 2001.

Riis, Jacob. *How the Other Half Lives.* Mineola, N.Y: Dover, 1971.

Serrin, Judith, and William Serrin (editors). *Muckraking! The Journalism That Changed America.* New York: The New Press, 2002.

Shapiro, Bruce. *Shaking the Foundations: 2,00 Years of Investigative Journalism in America.* New York: Avalon Publishing Group, 2003.

Sinclair, Upton. *The Autobiography of Upton Sinclair.* New York: Harcourt, Brace & World, Inc., 1962.

_____. *The Jungle: The Uncensored Original Edition.* Tucson, Ariz. See Sharp Press, 2003.

Steffens, Lincoln. *The Autobiography of Lincoln Steffens.* New York: Harcourt, Brace and Company, Inc., 1931.

_____. *The Shame of the Cities.* Original publication, New York: McClure, Phillips & Co., 1904; Reproduced, Mineola, N.Y: Dover Publications, Inc., 2004.

Tarbell, Ida M. *All in the Day's Work: An Autobiography.* New York: The Macmillan Company, 1939.

_____. *The History of the Standard Oil Company* (briefer version). Edited by David M. Chalmers. New York Harper & Row, 1966; Reproduced, Mineola, N.Y: Dover Publications, Inc., 2003.

Weinberg, Arthur, and Lila Weinberg (editors). *The Muckrakers.* Urbana: University of Illinois Press, 2001.

Wilson, Harold S. *McClure's Magazine and the Muckrakers.* Princeton, N.J.: Princeton University Press, 1970.

Woodward, Bob. *The Secret Man: The Story of Watergate's Deep Throat.* New York: Simon & Schuster, 2005.

Research Notes and Acknowledgments

RESEARCH NOTES: Much reading and some travel form the background for this work. An early trip to western Pennsylvania—including a visit to Ida Tarbell's childhood hometown (where her house still stands), her alma mater, her grave, and sites of importance to her family and others during the region's oil boom—helped set the stage for my research of the period. I am grateful to Jane F. Westenfeld, librarian for Special Collections of Pelletier Library at Allegheny College in Meadville, and Susan Beates, archivist at the Drake Well Museum near Titusville, for opening their collections of documents and photographs to me during this trip. Most memorable is a fall drive made on now-silent roads that once hummed with industry, including a gravel path along a tributary to Oil Creek that was frequented by Tarbell's father and is still littered with the ghostly relics of abandoned oil derricks, pipelines, and tanks.

Other travels took me to Washington, D.C., where I spent days combing through turn-of-the-20th-century photographs of meatpacking (never before lunch), other muckraking topics, key journalists and journals, and period cartoons at the Prints and Photographs Collections of the Library of Congress. Images from these collections enrich this book immeasurably. I visited the Rockefeller Archive Center at Pocantico Hills in Sleepy Hollow, N.Y., to gain my own sense of John D. Rockefeller, Sr., and I thank Ken Rose for graciously opening the family collections to me for an afternoon of photo and archival research. I'm grateful for a day spent immersed in bound volumes of *McClure's* Magazine—original newsstand issues with their covers and advertisements intact, a rare find—at the New-York Historical Society in New York City, as well.

Then there were the books! My writing-based topic led me to four kinds of reading. First, of course, were the period pieces of muckraking themselves, and I read extensive excerpts from Ida Tarbell's *The History of the Standard*

Oil Company, Lincoln Steffens's *The Shame of the Cities,* and (in its entirety) the original serial version of Upton Sinclair's *The Jungle*—the key works by the three featured authors in this study. Second came autobiographies, and every muckraker seems to have written at least one. All the ones I sampled—from Steffens to Tarbell to Sinclair to Ray Stannard Baker to S.S. McClure himself (with ghostwriting assistance from Willa Cather)—made for exceptional reading. Each author incorporated such recall (no doubt assisted by personal journals) that the books are bursting with detail and color from the period. I used these works to re-create the scene at *McClure's Magazine* and to complete the three chapters on muckraking assignments.

I read scholarly assessments of the muckraking era and the history of journalism, and these became an important third component of my research. Of particular assistance were Harold S. Wilson's *McClure's Magazine and the Muckrakers* and *The Muckrake Years* by David Mark Chalmers. *Voices of a Nation,* by Jean Folkerts and Dwight L. Teeter, Jr., provided important background information, particularly for Chapter 3. The multivolume biography of Theodore Roosevelt by Edmund Morris provided insights into Roosevelt's background in reform, his Presidency during the muckraker era, and his "Man with the Muckrake" speech (Chapter 5). Ron Chernow's *Titan: The Life of John D. Rockefeller, Sr.,* helped me understand Rockefeller's view of Tarbell's work.

Finally, there are many anthologies of muckraking (some of which are broadly defined to include works from the 19th century through contemporary times) that provide convenient access to examples of investigative journalism with accompanying analysis and background. I used these secondary resources to introduce other muckrakers into the book, provide historical context to the period (for example, outlining the reforms that followed different muckraker topics), and establish a sense of the enduring tradition of investigative journalism (Chapter 6 and the time line). The accompanying bibliography presents a comprehensive listing of all consulted resources.

ACKNOWLEDGMENTS: This project closes with a most pleasant assignment—the opportunity to acknowledge, in addition to the authors, archivists, and research institutions noted above, my sincere appreciation to the many individuals who stand behind this book. Above all I thank my husband, Dan, and my sons, Sam and Jake, who watch my writing become all-consuming at times, and yet welcome me back at home and table whether I've been transported away in my mind or through my feet. Thank you.

My parents, brother, other family members, and friends deserve credit for being equally understanding and supportive. I owe thanks to my brother-in-law and his family for sharing their second home with me at just the right time for some crucial writing—and throwing in up-north scenery and a lake to boot.

Then there are my friends in the world of books to thank—from readers to librarians to other authors, including the unstoppable members of my critique group. Most important of all are the people at National Geographic Children's Books who've believed in my work from the exchange of our first post, and especially Jennifer Emmett who has been my editor from that moment on. She is unflappable, gracious, humorous, and wise; I have no fears or worries with her on my side. Thank you for making it possible for me to write this book. My appreciation goes to her supportive colleagues, too, including Nancy Laties Feresten, Mary Beth Oelkers-Keegan, Lori Epstein, and Bea Jackson. Special thanks are due Marty Ittner for dreaming up the inspired design that enriches this book.

No acknowledgments would be complete without commending those journalists who inspired this work and without whom our lives would undoubtedly be diminished. May the story of their labors and triumphs inspire the next generation of muckraking. Write on!

***

Ann Bausum brings history alive for children through her meticulous research and compelling narrative. *Muckrakers* is Ann's sixth book for the National Geographic Society. Other titles include *Freedom Riders, With Courage and Cloth,* and *Our Country's Presidents.* Ann lives in Beloit, Wisconsin, with her husband and two teenage sons. To find out more about her writing, visit her on the Web at www.AnnBausum.com.

Daniel Schorr has had an award-winning career in journalism that spans more than six decades. Highlights include his 1957 exclusive interview with Soviet leader Nikita Krushchev while a foreign correspondent for CBS and his stint as chief Watergate correspondent for CBS, where his coverage earned him three Emmys. Currently he is a senior news analyst for National Public Radio. His memoir is *Staying Tuned: A Life in Journalism.*

Citations and Illustrations Credits

Abbreviations used below are IMT (Ida M. Tarbell), JDR John D. Rockefeller, Sr.), LS (Lincoln Steffens), RSB (Ray Stannard Baker), SSM (Samuel Sidney McClure), TR (Theodore Roosevelt), and US (Upton Sinclair).

Introduction

RAISED QUOTE: RSB: "The journalist is a true servant of democracy...." (Wilson: p.285).

Chapter 1—The Shame of the Nation

RAISED QUOTE: LS: "If I should be entrusted with the work I think I could make my name." (Tarbell, 1939: p.201).
TEXT: SSM: "Get out, go anywhere, everywhere...." (Tarbell, 1939: p.200); LS recollection: "as if pursued." (Steffens, 1931: p.368); Joseph W. Folk: "beyond belief." (Steffens, 1931: p.368); LS recollection: "left out some

salient facts.... take the blame." (Steffens, 1931: p.372-73); LS: "Evidently you could shoot me out of a gun...." (Steffens, 1931: p.392); IMT: "No response—no more chapters...." (Tarbell, 1939: p.202) excerpt from "The Shamelessness of St. Louis": "government of the people, by the rascals, for the rich." (Steffens 2004: p.70).

Chapter 2—Muckraker Origins

RAISED QUOTE SSM: "When Mr. Steffens, Mr. Baker, Miss Tarbell write..." (Wilson: pp. 195-96).

PHOTO CAPTIONS: SSM: "I can't sit still...." (Steffens, 1931: p.362).

TEXT: LS: "with his valise full of clippings...." (Steffens, 1931: pp. 362-63); RSB: "He was all intuition and impulse...." (Baker: p.95) IMT: *McClure's* could "no longer be content...." (Tarbell, 1939: p.196); SSM: "a coincidence that may set us thinking" and other excerpts from January 1903 editorial *(McClure's Magazine,* Vol.30, No.3, p.336); RSB: "If I got mad, you wouldn't...." (Wilson:

pp. 191-92); SSM: "If we let in light and air...." (Wilson: p.204).

Chapter 3—Fighting the Octopus

RAISED QUOTE: IMT: "[Standard Oil] had never played fair...." (Tarbell, 1939: p.230).

TEXT: Frank Tarbell (IMT's father): "Don't do it, Ida—they will ruin the magazine." (Tarbell, 1939: p.207); IMT personal correspondence: "appalling heaps of documentary stuff" (Wilson, 1970: p.141); IMT: "It was worth the trip." (Allegheny College archives, Tarbell's typed notes) Ron Chernow: She wrote "in the dispassionate manner associated with McClure's...." (Chernow: p.443); JDR: "Not a word...." (Tarbell, 1939: p.239); JDR: "It has always been the policy of the Standard...." (Tarbell, 1939: p.239); Ron Chernow: Tarbell's work "turned America's most private man...." (Chernow: p.438); SSM: "40 or 50 odd little republics" (Wilson: p.225); IMT: "I accuse Mr. Rockefeller...." (Wilson, 1970: p.306).

Chapter 4—Labor and Lamb Chops

RAISED QUOTE verse, *New York Evening Post.* (Crunden: p.174).

PHOTO CAPTIONS: *The Jungle:* "All the barnyards of the universe.... It would have taken all day simply to count the pens." (Sinclair, 2003: p.27); *The Jungle:* "everything about the pig except the squeal." (Sinclair, 2003: p.28).

TEXT: US: "I went about white-faced and thin...." (Sinclair, 1962: p.109); excerpt from *The Jungle:* "Murder it was that went on there.... turning them into dollars and cents." (Sinclair, 2003: p.82); Jack London: "Dear Comrades: Here it is at last! ... Yours for the revolution, Jack London." (Eby: pp. 485-86); Robert M. Crunden: The public "took a book of well over 300 pages...." (Crunden: p.173); TR: "to regulate interstate commerce...." (Eby: p.379); Ogden Armour: "yellow journalism." (Eby) US: "I aimed at the public's heart...." (Eby: p.351).

Chapter 5—Shaking the Foundations

RAISED QUOTE: TR: "If the whole picture is painted black...." (Weinberg: p.60). photo captions David Graham Phillips: "Judge public men by what they do and are, not by what they say and pretend." (Weinberg: p.60).

TEXT: TR: "Put sky in the landscape." (Wilson: p.179); TR: "Tell Sinclair to go home...." (Sinclair, 1963: p.124); excerpts from TR's "muckraker speech" of April 14, 1906 (Weinberg: pp.58-65); Robert M. Crunden: "The progressive President..." (Crunden: p.192); LS: "Well, you've put an end...." (Weinberg: p.57); IMT: "misread his Bunyan." (Tarbell, 1939: p.242); *The Pilgrim's Progress:* "straws, and sticks, and dust." (Bunyan: p.207); IMT: TR believed that reform "should be left to him.... stealing his thunder." (Tarbell, 1939: p.242); *American Magazine* announcement. (Baker, 1945: p.226-27); RSB: the days "when we were both saving the world.... how hard boiled it was." (Wilson: p.321).

Chapter 6—An Enduring Tradition

RAISED QUOTE: Jessica Mitford: "You may not be able to change the world...." Jensen: p.151).

PHOTO CAPTIONS: Edward R. Murrow: "We must not confuse dissent with disloyalty.... deserting it at home." (Jensen: p.144).

TEXT: reputation of Edward R. Murrow's March 9, 1954 *See It Now* program as "television's finest hour." (Jensen: p.138); RSB: "I suppose they will return again.... almost a mission and a call." (Wilson: p.322).

Afterword

RAISED QUOTE: IMT: "I realized early that what a man or a woman does...." (Tarbell, 1939: p.400).

TEXT: Drew Pearson: "It is the job of a newspaperman...." (Serrin: p.119); Robert C. Kochersberger, Jr.: "The group changed things...." (Kochersberger: p.xxii); IMT: "We all sat down together...." (Tarbell, 1939: p.406) Ron Chernow: *History of the*

Standard Oil Company "remains one of the great case studies...." (Chernow: p.) IMT: "Not one word, young man, not one word." (Brady: p.160); Charles Edward Russell: "There is no such thing in this world...." (Weinberg: p.435).

Pantheon of Muckrakers

TEXT: Nellie Bly: "Energy rightly applied...." (Kroeger: p.85); Jacob Riis: "The sea of a mighty population...." (Riis: p.229); Ida B. Wells-Barnett: "I'd rather go down in history...." (Library of Congress poster caption: LC-USZ62-102002); p, 96, SSM: "People often ask me how I got ideas...." (McClure: p.247); LS: "You may beat the public to the news...." (Steffens, 1931: p.394); IMT: "There was born in me a hatred of privilege...." (Tarbell, 1939: p.26) RSB: "We were ourselves personally astonished...." (Baker: p.183); US: "I have reformed three American families..." *(New York World-Telegram & Sun:* Oct.29, 196[3?]); US: "I don't know whether anyone will care to examine..." (Sinclair, 1962: p.329); Edward R. Murrow: "We will not walk in fear, one of another...." (Jensen: p.144); 101, Rachel Carson: "No witchcraft, no enemy action...." (Jensen: p.124); Bob Woodward: "There are always unanswered questions...." (Woodward: p.219); Carl Bernstein: "Reporters may believe they control the story...." (Woodward: p.224); Seymour Hersh: "You have to not be afraid to tell the truth." Jensen: p.237).

Illustrations Credits

Grateful acknowledgment is made for the use of images from the following sources. Abbreviations used below are IMTC (Ida M. Tarbell Collection, Special Collections, Pelletier Library, Allegheny College), LC (courtesy the Library of Congress Prints and Photographs Division), LL (courtesy the Lilly Library, Indiana University, Bloomington, Indiana), and NYHS (Collection of the New-York Historical Society).Front cover, clockwise from upper left, LC-USZ62-53912, LC-DIG-ggbain-00788, LC-DIG-ggbain-05710 courtesy Richard Polt courtesy of Daniel Schorr LC-USZ62-93125 NYHS #49661

LC-USZ62-75558 LC-USZ62-57594 LL
LC-USZ62-29057 LC-B2-2765-12 LL
IMTC #250; IMTC #16p;
LC-USZ62-63520; LC-USZCN4-122,
courtesy of the Rockefeller Archive
Center LC-USZ62-132336,
LC-USZ62-38388, LC-USZ62-114375,
LC-USZ62-50217, upper,
LC-USZCN4-166, lower,
LC-USZ62-55406, LC-USZ62-95886,
LC-USZ62-129006, LC-USZ62-58861,
courtesy the University of Illinois Press,
LC-USZ62-64261, IMTC #3901,
LC-USZ62-126483, LC-L9-54-3252,
LC-USZ62-111207, Bettmann/CORBIS
Bettmann/CORBIS clockwise from left,
LC-DIG-ggbain-18151,
LC-USZ62-100905, NYHS #44853
LC-USZ62-41374, LC-DIG-ggbain-18165,
Bettmann/CORBIS LC-USZ62-59924,
upper, LC-USZ62-113814, lower, Getty
Images LC-DIG-ggbain-05453,
upper-LC-DIG-ggbain-05710, lower,
LC-USZ62-117943, LC-USZ62-36754,
LC-DIG-ggbain-00788,
LC-USZ62-107889, LC-USZ62-107991,
Bettmann/CORBIS Bettmann/CORBIS;
back cover, courtesy the University of
Illinois Press. Istockphoto.com provided

all typewriter keys, the notebook paper used for raised quotes, and the antique postcard printed behind each profile in the Pantheon of Muckrakers.

**Published by the
National Geographic Society**
John M. Fahey, Jr.,
President and Chief Executive Officer
Gilbert M. Grosvenor,
Chairman of the Board
Nina D. Hoffman, *Executive Vice President;
President, Book Publishing Group*

Staff for This Book
Nancy Laties Feresten, *Vice President, Editor-in-Chief of Children's Books*
Bea Jackson, *Design and illustrations Director, Children's Books*
Jennifer Emmett, Mary Beth Oelkers-Keegan, *Project Editors*
Lori Epstein, *illustrations Editor*
Carl Mehler, *Director of Maps*
Marry Ittner, *Designer*
Rebecca Baines, *Editorial Assistant*
Barbara L. Klein, *Copyeditor and Researcher*
Connie D. Binder, *Indexer*
R. Gary Colbert, *Production Director*
Lewis R. Bassford, *Production Manager*
Maryclare Tracy, Nicole Elliott, *Manufacturing Managers*

The publisher wishes to thank Robert D. Johnston, Ph.D., University of Illinois, for his expert review.

Founded in 1888, the National Geographic Society is one of the largest nonprofit scientific and educational organizations in the world. It reaches more than 285 million people worldwide each month through its official journal, National Geographic, and its four other magazines; the National Geographic Channel; television documentaries; radio programs; films; books; videos and DVDs; maps; and interactive media. National Geographic has funded more than 8,000 scientific research projects and supports an education program combating geographic illiteracy.

For more information, please call 1-800-NGS LINE (647-5463) or write to the following address:

National Geographic Society

1145 17th Street N.W.
Washington, D.G. 20036-4688 U.S.A.

Visit us online at www.nationalgeographic.com/books

For information about special discounts for bulk purchases, please contact National Geographic Books Special Sales: ngspecsales@ngs.org

Front Cover Flap

Political corruption, corporate greed, sickness and death from tainted foods—today's headlines may shock us, but in fact they echo the scandalous exposés of the past century. Then, as now, it was the news media—not government agencies, not lawyers, and not politicians—who frequently brought the truth to light.

Journalism has been dubbed the unofficial fourth branch of government, serving as the watchdog of the executive, legislative, and judicial branches and helping to rebalance the division of power when things get out of whack. Using their constitutional freedom of the press, journalists investigate, expose, and urge reform. They give voice to the concerns of citizens and shed light on the nation's faults.

In the early 20th century, when investigative journalism was just getting started, Ida Tarbell exposed the spreading tentacles of the monopoly of Standard Oil, while Upton Sinclair portrayed the unseemly realities of high-volume meatpacking, and Lincoln Steffens blew the lid off civic corruption. Theodore Roosevelt dubbed such writers "muckrakers" because he felt many of them had crossed the line of decency and were only raking up "muck"—dirt, wrongdoing, and scandal. His negative term stuck even as investigative writing continued.

Award-winning author Ann Bausum's sweeping narrative paints a vivid picture of the American news media during the Regressive era, showing how muckrakers created an essential democratic tradition that endures to this day.

Daniel Schorr has had an award-winning career in journalism that spans more than six decades. Highlights include his 1957 exclusive interview with Soviet leader Nikita Krushchev while a foreign correspondent for CBS and his stint as chief Watergate correspondent for CBS, where his coverage earned him three Emmys. Currently he is a senior news analyst for National Public Radio. His memoir is *Staying Tuned: A Life in Journalism.*

Back Cover Flap

"Bausum ... makes the history live as she explains, exhorts, and lets nothing drop by the wayside.... Excellent."—*Kirkus, Starred Review, With Courage and Cloth*

Ann Bausum is an award-winning children's book author who came of age when journalists fought for the right to publish the Pentagon Papers, and Woodward and Bernstein exposéd the Watergate scandal. "These writers were my childhood heroes," she notes. "Their nose for a good story and relentless pursuit of the truth helped change the course of history." Ann uses this same approach—pains-taking research, an eye for just the right illustration, and the ability to tie it all together in a compelling narrative—to bring history alive for young people.

Muckrakers is Ann's sixth book for the National Geographic Society. Other titles include Our Country's Presidents, *Our Country's First Ladies, and Dragon Bones and Dinosaur Eggs: A Photobiography of Explorer Roy*

Chapman Andrews. Ann lives in Beloit, Wisconsin, with her husband and two teenage sons. To find out more about her writing, visit her on the Web at www.AnnBausum.com.

Look for these other books by Ann Bausum about people who made a difference in American history:
- Winner of the Jane Addams Children's Book Award for Older Readers
- An ALA Notable Book and an ALA Best Book for Young Adults
- *A School Library Journal* Best Book of the Year
- New York Public Library 100 Titles for Reading and Sharing
- New York Public Library Books for the Teen Age

"Another excellent work of nonfiction ... delivers a galvanizing call to action."—*Booklist, Starred Review*

"Bausum's narrative style ... fresh, engrossing, and at times heart-stopping ... will draw readers in and keep them captivated."—*School Library Journal, Starred Review*

- Robert F. Sibert Informational Book Honor

- A *Booklist* Top of the List Year's Best Youth Nonfiction

Back Cover Material

Reform-minded writers of the early 20th century stirred up the storm clouds of "popular indignation" with their investigations. This public outcry spurred President Theodore Roosevelt to attack the exposéd scandal and muck—and to condemn the journalists, saying they had gone too far.

This book is about the power of language.

It's about the quest by news writers to uncover the truth, not just report surface fact.

It's about having the vision—and patience—to study a clouded picture until the full view comes into focus

It's about words that change a nation.

Index

A
Abu Ghraib prison, Iraq, 83
Advertising, 69, 75, 83
African-Americans, 12
Appeal to Reason, 39, 44, 45
Armour, Ogden, 51
Automobile industry, 77, 79

B
Baker, Ray Stannard,
  on The American Magazine staff, 67, 69
  later life, 69
  muckraking, 22, 64, 69
  thoughts about muckraking, 67, 69, 83
Bernstein, Carl, 79, 82
Black Americans, 12
Bly, Nellie, 22, 26
Books, muckraking, 77, 79
Boyden, Albert, 69
Bunyan, John, 45, 60, 63, 64
Businesses,
  ruthlessness, 22, 26, 28, 29, 31, 33, 36
  treatment of workers, 16, 39
Butler, Ed, 1, 4

C
Carson, Rachel, 77, 79, 82
Chicago, Illinois, meatpacking industry, 39, 41, 44, 45, 48, 49, 51
Corruption, government, 1, 3, 4, 7, 8, 12, 13, 16, 17, 18
Cosmopolitan Magazine,

Treason of the Senate series, *56, 57, 60*
Crunden, Robert M., *49, 62*

F
Factories, working conditions, *26, 39*
Folk, Joseph, *1, 3*
Food safety, legislation, *51*
Funeral industry, *77, 79*

G
Ghernow, Ron, *33*
Glaberson, William, *83*
Golden Rule, *28, 29, 36*

H
Harrington, Michael, *77, 79*
Hersh, Seymour, *79, 82, 83*

I
Internet, muckraking, *83*
Iraq War, *82, 83*
injured soldiers, *83*
prisoners, *83*

J
Journalism,

L
Laborers, unions, *22, 28*
working conditions, *39, 45, 49, 73, 75, 82*
La Follette, Robert, *67*
Legislation, *77, 79*
Lincoln, Abraham, *18, 29*
London, Jack, *45, 48*

M
McCarthy, Joseph, *75, 77*
McClure, Samuel Sidney, *18, 22, 26*
conflict with staff, *64, 66*
enthusiasm, *1, 18, 26*

as muckraking publisher, *4, 18, 20, 22, 33, 56, 67*
philosophy, *22, 29*
salaries paid to writers, *20, 31*
McClure's Magazine, circulation, *31, 67*
civic responsibility, *18, 20*
muckraking articles, *1, 3, 4, 7, 8, 12, 13, 16, 17, 18, 28, 29, 31, 64, 67*
staff, *1, 64, 66, 67, 69*
writing style, *22, 29, 31*
Meatpacking industry, *39, 41, 44, 45, 48, 49, 51*
Medicines, poisonous, *60*
Migrant workers, *73, 75*
Mitford, Jessica, *75, 77, 79*
Monopolies, *28, 36*
Montessori, Maria, *67*
Movies, *75, 82*
Muckrakers,
advice for, *75*
coining of term, *60, 62, 63*
cycles, *73*
influence, *77, 79*
origins, *12, 13, 16, 17, 18, 20, 22, 26, 28, 29*
recent, *82, 83*
skills, *73*
Murrow, Edward R., *73, 75, 77*

N
Nader, Ralph, *77, 79*
Nixon, Richard M., *82*
Norr, Roy, *75*

O
Oil industry, *26, 28, 29, 31, 33, 36*

P
Pentagon Papers, *79*
Pesticides, *77, 82*

Phillips, David Graham, *56, 57, 60*
Phillips, John S., *69*
Poverty, *26, 77, 79*
Priest, Dana, *83*
Prisoners of war, *83*
Progressive era, *18, 69*
Pulitzer Prizes, *75, 82*
Pure Food and Drug Act of 1906, *51*

R
Reader's Digest, *75*
Riis, Jacob, *26*
Rockefeller, John D., Sr., *22, 26, 28, 31, 33, 36*
Roosevelt, Franklin Delano, *69, 73*
Roosevelt, Theodore, *56*
   anger with muckrakers, *8, 56, 57, 60, 62*
   defining muckraker journalism, *64, 67, 69*
   elections, *60, 69*
   encouraging muckrakers, *18, 56*
   reforms, *26, 33, 36, 51, 62, 63, 64*

S
Sanger, Margaret, *73*
Schlosser, Eric, *82*
Seldes, George, *75*
Sheehan, Neil, *79*
Sherman Antitrust Act of 1890, *36*
Siddall, John, *69*
Silent Spring (Carson), *77, 79, 82*
Sinclair, Upton, *39*
   early life, *39*
   later years, *83*
   meatpacking industry exposé, *39, 41, 44, 45, 48, 49, 51, 56, 73*
Smoking, dangers, *75*
Socialism, *39, 45, 48, 51, 62*
Spanish-American War, *13*

St. Louis, Missouri,
political
corruption, *1, 3, 4*
streetcars, *4*
Standard Oil
Company, *22, 26, 28, 33, 36*
   cartoon, *29*
Steffen, Lincoln, *69*
   and Jacob Riis, *13, 26*
   criticism of
Roosevelt's
muckraker
speech, *62*
   and Jacob Riis, *13, 26*
   later life, *69, 83*
   memoirs, *67, 69*
   reporting on
government
corruption, *1, 3, 4, 7, 8, 20, 67*
Steinbeck, John, *73, 75*

T

The American
Magazine, *66, 67*
   staff, *69*
The Grapes of
Wrath (Steinbeck), *73, 75*
The Jungle
(Sinclair), *41, 45, 48, 49, 51, 73, 75, 77*
The New York
Times, *79, 83*
The Pilgrim's
Progress (Bunyan), *28, 45, 60, 63, 64*
Taft, William
Howard, *69*
Tarbell, Franklin
Sumner, *26, 28*
Tarbell, Ida, *26, 69*
   on The American
Magazine staff, *67, 69*
   autobiography, *31, 63, 64*
   criticism of
Roosevelt's
muckraker
speech, *63, 64*
   early life, *26, 29*
   later life, *69, 83*

Standard Oil Company exposé, *26, 28, 29, 31, 33, 36*
Television, muckraking, *75, 77*
Torture, *83*
The Washington Post, *79, 82, 83*

U
U.S. Constitution,
First Amendment, *79*
definition of treason, *57*
selection of Senators, *56*
U.S. Senate,
corruption, *56, 57, 63*
pesticide hearings, *82*
selection process, *56*
U.S. Supreme Court,
Pentagon Papers decision, *79*

V
Vietnam War, *79*

W
Walter Reed Army Medical Center, *83*
Watergate break-in, *79, 82*
Wells-Barnett, Ida B., *26*
Wilson, Woodrow, *69*
Woodward, Bob, *79, 82*
Working conditions, *16, 39, 45, 49, 73, 75, 82*
World War I, *69*

Y
Yellow journalism, *12*

www.ingramcontent.com/pod-product-compliance
Lightning Source LLC
Chambersburg PA
CBHW011737220426
43661CB00062B/2876